LIMITLESS

Jentezen Franklin

CHARISMA
HOUSE

Cover design by Justin Evans

Visit the author's website at www.jentezenfranklin.org.

Library of Congress Cataloging-in-Publication Data:
Names: Franklin, Jentezen, 1962- author.
Title: Limitless / by Jentezen Franklin.
Other titles: Spirit of python
Description: Lake Mary : Charisma House, 2016. |
Originally published under
   title: The spirit of python : Lake Mary, FL : Charisma
House, 2013. |
   Includes bibliographical references and index.
Identifiers: LCCN 2015051234 (print) | LCCN 2016005300
(ebook) | ISBN
   9781629986654 (trade paper : alk. paper) | ISBN
9781629986661 (e-book)
Subjects: LCSH: Spiritual warfare. | Devil.
Classification: LCC BV4509.5 .F7463 2016 (print) | LCC
BV4509.5 (ebook) | DDC
   235/.4--dc23
LC record available at http://lccn.loc.gov/2015051234

This book was adapted from *The Spirit of Python* by
Jentezen Franklin, published by Charisma House Book
Group, ISBN 978-1-62136-220-3, copyright © 2013.

16 17 18 19 20 — 987654321
Printed in the United States of America

CONTENTS

INTRODUCTION

WHEN IT SEEMS as if everything is falling apart, it can be hard to stay focused on the promises of God. With the weight of the world on your shoulders it becomes very inviting to sit down and give up. Before you know it, doubt, frustration, and bitterness begin to creep in and steal all of the joy and power from your life and your relationship with God.

You have a real enemy that battles for your soul and his name is Satan. The good news is that you don't have to live a powerless Christian life. You don't have to listen to the negative voices in your head that say things are never going to get better or that this is all you'll ever be. You don't have to believe that your kids are never going to serve God or you'll never regain your health.

As followers of Christ we don't have to live with hopelessness, depression, or addiction. We don't have to live powerless, lukewarm Christian lives. We can be victorious through the power of the Holy Spirit!

You *can* expect God to come through! God has made provision for victory and power in your Christian life. Your present circumstances do not have to limit your faith or dictate your future. You can live the life He planned for you: a limitless life!

This is more than positive thinking. It is a passionate challenge to live a life of zero tolerance for sin, distractions, or lies from the enemy, and to boldly and obediently to step into a new season of life where God makes all things new and the limitations of the past become a distant memory.

It's time to let go of the baggage and overcome the limits of your past once and for all. Block the enemy's access into your life and cancel his assignments to limit you. Revive your prayer life and worship times through new levels of intimacy with God. Activate your faith to stop merely talking about miracles and start experiencing them. Dream God-sized dreams, determine not to become satisfied with less than God's best, and decide to go to the next level in your walk with God.

As you read the powerful insights from the Lord in the pages that follow, you will find strategies for overcoming the enemy's attacks and will learn to walk in victory, dismantling Satan's schemes in your life and loosening his grip on you so that you can live a life of abundance as God intends.

Chapter One

LIVE VICTORIOUSLY

IMAGINE YOURSELF IN the Desert of Judea at the edge of the Jordan River. John the Baptist, the first prophetic voice from God to speak in four hundred years, has been preaching repentance in the desert. He is a wild-haired young man, dressed in animal skins and subsisting on locusts and wild honey. Many recognize him as the one spoken of by the Prophet Isaiah—"A voice cries out in the desert: 'Prepare the way for the Lord! Make his paths straight!'" (Matt. 3:3, GW). You, like so many others from Jerusalem and all of Judea and the whole region of the Jordan, are coming out to the desert to confess your sins and be baptized by John. As he preaches, John tells of one who is coming, one who will be much more powerful and will baptize with the Holy Spirit and fire!

Then you notice a man coming through the crowd. He approaches John at the water's edge, asking to be baptized. John hesitates, saying, "You need to baptize me," but the man insists, knowing it is the will of God

1

in order that all righteousness can be fulfilled. And so John consents and baptizes Him. As the man [Jesus] comes up out of the water, the whole of the Trinity is present. The Holy Spirit of God descends from heaven and rests upon Jesus, and God speaks, declaring that Jesus is "my Son, whom I love; with him I am well pleased" (Matt. 3:17, NIV). Like everyone around you, you are speechless. Something very holy has just occurred but you aren't sure what it all means.

With this glorious event the public ministry of Jesus begins. But Jesus doesn't stride away from the riverbank and begin to heal and teach about the kingdom of God. Instead, He allows Himself to be led by the Spirit of God into the desert to be tempted by the devil. For forty days He fasts. We can only imagine how weak in body and mind He must have become.

Then, on the fortieth day the devil comes. The Bible calls him "the tempter." He has come to see if he can dislodge Jesus from His mission. First, he appeals to Jesus's physical hunger, but Jesus rebuffs him with the Word of God. Next, Satan tries to challenge Jesus's identity, tempting Him to use supernatural powers. "*If* You are the Son of God," he says, "then demonstrate it! Throw Yourself from the high point of the temple." Again Jesus rebuffs him with Scripture, telling the devil that it is God we must rely on. Then the devil comes at Him one more time, tempting Jesus to worship him (Satan). "Away from me, Satan!" cries Jesus. "For it is written: 'Worship the Lord your God, and serve him only'" (Matt. 4:10, NIV). With that, the devil slinks away.

In this account of the temptation of Jesus, we find the foundation—the blueprint—given to us by Jesus for victorious living. Scripture doesn't pull any punches here. We *will* be tempted by the devil in this life, but Jesus has modeled how we can live a life of victory in the midst of the devil's attacks. He, Jesus, has won the victory and because of that we don't have to allow Satan to run rampant in our lives. When the pressures of family, work, finances, or health feel as if they are going to overwhelm us, we need to press into the One who has overcome instead of trying to rectify things through our own efforts. We need to learn how to live according to the Spirit of God through Christ in us, the hope of glory.

Walk Fully in Your Identity in Christ

God's Word tells us it's not by might or by power, but by His Spirit that we advance the kingdom (Zech. 4:6). In the power of God's spirit we can boldly and obediently step into a new season of life where God makes all things new, and the limitations of the past become a distant memory; where there is zero tolerance for sin, distractions, or the lies of the enemy. God doesn't intend for you to just read about miracles. He wants you to experience them, to dream God-sized dreams, to live powerfully and passionately for Christ and His kingdom every day.

You will recall that in Genesis, God breathed the breath of life into Adam, and Adam became a living soul. In John 20:22 Jesus breathed on His disciples and said, "Receive the Holy Spirit" (MEV.) In Acts 2 the Holy Spirit came as a mighty rushing wind. Breath, air, and wind are symbols of the Holy Spirit in Scripture, and guess who's trying to choke and suffocate the breath (life) out of believers? That's right—Satan! Satan is after one thing; he is trying to extract the breath and the anointing of the Holy Spirit from our lives because without the power and anointing of the Holy Spirit we cannot do anything with lasting effect.

Jesus Himself warned us that the devil only comes to steal, kill, and destroy (John 10:10), calling the devil a murderer and the father of lies (John 8:44). In the Book of Revelation John called him an old serpent who deceives the whole world (Rev. 12:9). Satan first showed up in the Garden of Eden in the form of a serpent, and he has been busy ever since trying to destroy the people of God. While we are not to overemphasize the work of the devil, we need to know who our adversary is and understand his ways so that we can fight him on God's terms—with the power of God!

For the body of Christ there has never been a more crucial time for us to wake up and know Jesus, the One who lives within us in the power of the Spirit. As followers of Christ we can be victorious. God will come through for us, and we should expect no less of Him. He wants us to live the life He planned for us—a limitless life.

Know Who You Are Fighting

In the Book of Acts, Paul and Silas were confronted by a slave girl with a spirit by which she predicted the future (Acts 16:16). This particular type of demonic spirit was known as a python spirit. Those possessed by this kind of spirit were known to speak involuntarily. This girl followed Paul and Silas around, shouting until they became so tired of being heckled and mocked by the demon in her that they commanded it to come out of the girl, which it promptly did.

The problem was that this slave girl's ability to predict the future was a valuable asset to her owners, who became angry that she was no longer useful to them in that way. They incited a crowd against Paul and Silas and succeeded in getting them thrown in prison. This is but one example of Satan and his demons coming against Paul and the fledgling church, trying to choke the life out of the earliest believers.

The same spiritual force that came against Paul and the early church is still at work today, attacking believers in the twenty-first-century church. Instead of being overcomers Christians are allowing themselves to be overcome. Just as Paul and Silas were on their way to the place of prayer when Satan interrupted them, Satan will try and do the same to you. Every time you try and draw near to the Father, the devil will go on the defensive to thwart your efforts. If Satan can't stop you from receiving Christ as your Savior, then hell has a Plan B, which is to make you a passionless, powerless Christian.   — full worm

Take Hold of God's Provision

If we read a little further in chapter 16 of the Book of Acts, we find Paul and Silas at midnight, singing praises after being arrested and beaten and thrown in prison. Midnight in the Scriptures is sometimes an analogy for the coming of the Lord, or the last days. What Scripture is telling us is that Satan tried to stop Paul and Silas just before God showed up in their lives (at midnight). But these two men were undeterred because they knew that they could overcome by the power of God's Spirit within them, and so as an act of spiritual warfare, they sang praise songs and prayed and were able to defeat Satan's plans. Their story reveals a lot about why prayer, praise, and the power and presence of the Holy Spirit are vital to our spiritual life—and why these are the very things the enemy seeks to choke out of us.

We must make no mistake—the battle between light and darkness is very real. If Satan can't stop you from receiving Christ as your Savior, then he will try and slowly use temptations, cares, pressures, and burdens to squeeze the joy out of your walk with the Lord. The good news is that you have the power to defeat Satan, and this book contains some deep spiritual insights I believe the Lord gave me to help you understand how to do just that. In the pages that follow, we are going to take a look at the key weapons in your spiritual arsenal—specifically prayer, praise, and the spiritual armor of God.

Chapter Two

THINK PROACTIVELY

GOD WANTS US to think and live proactively, controlling situations by bringing His kingdom to bear rather than responding to an attack of Satan after it's happened. But in order to respond proactively to Satan's attacks, we need to recognize the warning signs. If you are outside and the sky grows dark, and the wind picks up, and the air turns cool and damp, you know that a storm is about to hit and you act accordingly. You recognize the warning signs and take appropriate action.

As believers we needn't be blindsided by spiritual attacks. When we recognize that Satan is on the move, we need to take appropriate action to thwart his efforts to inflict damage. While the goal of any spiritual attack is to turn us away from what God wants to do in our lives, the end result of our response is to keep us focused on what God is doing in our lives. Let's examine together some of the many ways in which Satan tries to turn us away from what God is doing in us and through us.

(handwritten margin note, rotated: Our response to the works of Satan in our lives.)

A Heart on Fire for God

God delights in us and He desires that we delight in Him. We are not to live by feelings alone, but to know the difference between doing something out of obligation and doing something because we delight in it. Hearts that delight in God are hearts on fire for Christ and His kingdom. When we delight in the Lord, nothing else compares. When we are passionate for God, we find pleasure in the things of God rather than the things of the world.

This kind of fire of the heart is known as spiritual desire, and Satan longs to cause us to lose our spiritual desire. He typically doesn't go about this in one fell swoop. Instead, he tries to slip into our lives unnoticed and slowly change our hearts, choking the breath of the Spirit out of us little by little until the fire goes out.

Have you ever felt just too busy to read your Bible so you don't? Or perhaps you are beginning to feel a disconnect when you pray, and before you know it, you spend less and less time in prayer until you just don't pray much at all anymore. Or maybe you find reasons not to go to church, allowing worldly pursuits to take the place of your pursuit of God, and pretty soon the fire in your heart has become barely lukewarm.

I'm not saying that we shouldn't do things we enjoy. It is fine to have hobbies, skills, sports, activities, and to travel. God wants us to live life abundantly. He just doesn't want worldly pursuits to squeeze out our relationship with Him. He wants to be part of every aspect of our lives. We have all seen Christians who were at one time passionate for the things of God begin to find all of their enjoyment in worldly things rather than the things of God. They failed to recognize the warning signs, allowing Satan to put out God's fire in their hearts.

RUN THE RACE WITH PERSEVERANCE

We are created beings, comprised of spirit, soul, and body. If our bodies are weak, things can get into our minds (souls) that negatively affect our spirits. This often comes by way of physical fatigue.

A good example of this kind of physical fatigue is found in Elijah after his run-in with Jezebel. After having fire fall from heaven and consume his offering, and then killing 850 of her prophets of Baal and Asherah, he delivered a sound blow to her kingdom. That had to be tiring, physically exhausting work, and that was when Jezebel attacked, sending a messenger to Elijah with her threat to kill him within twenty-four hours. Already worn down, he fled, traveling a full day into the wilderness. When the adrenaline finally wore off, he sat down under a tree and prayed that he would die (1 Kings 19:1–4), and then he fell asleep. After he rested awhile, an angel of the Lord awakened him and fed him.

After that tremendous victory, fatigue left Elijah feeling like a failure and open for attack. Like Elijah, many times we face our greatest attacks just before a great promotion or just after a great victory. Fatigue in the body wears on the mind. Our thoughts get twisted. <u>When you're going through an attack, remember that it could very well be an indication that you are about to be promoted or just had a great victory.</u> Press on through and God will meet you and provide for your needs just as He did for Elijah. As the writer of Hebrews said, "Therefore, since we are surrounded by such a great cloud of witnesses, let us throw off everything that hinders and the sin that so easily entangles. And let us run with perseverance the race marked out for us, fixing our eyes on Jesus, the pioneer and perfecter of faith" (Heb. 12:1–2, NIV).

Know the One Who Supplies All Our Needs

Most of us have experienced those times when it seems that all of our resources dry up at the same time, when everything starts breaking down all at once; when business dries up or layoffs are announced, the car breaks down, the appliances are on the fritz, and all the kids are sick. If you have experienced times like these, you could be under a "lack attack."

I have seen people who are fully committed to God

and are growing spiritually, then the enemy hits them with a lack attack. Suddenly their eyes are off of God and onto money. Along comes an opportunity, but not an anointed opportunity, and forgetting that not every "good" offer is from God, they start paying attention to the tempting offers from the devil. Satan has them worrying rather than worshipping, and they start making decisions based on opportunity instead of anointing. If you are going through a lack attack, focus your mind on God's promises, not on your problems.

Think about how Satan tried to sway Jesus from His purpose, offering Him all the kingdoms of the world and a way out of the cross. Of course, there was a catch. The devil added, "All these things I will give You *if* You will fall down and worship me" (Matt. 4:9, MEV, emphasis added). Make no mistake, the devil will orchestrate circumstances to give you what you are looking for at a vulnerable moment in your life and then steal from you what matters most.

In order to discern whether you are making a decision based on opportunity or anointing, ask yourself questions such as, "Does the financial solution pull me away from God's house on Sunday?" "Does it take me away from family?" "Am I training a generation to take their life direction from money rather than trusting God?"

Of course it is important that we work—but when our jobs take us away from the things of God, it is

When faced with decisions

likely that we have traded the things of God for money. If young people want to work, that is great. But the job needs to allow them to go to church, to have time for God. Never let your kids trade the things of God for minimum wage. The new phone, better car, or cooler jeans are just not worth that much in light of eternity.

Remember, there are two times in life when you are especially vulnerable to temptation: when you have nothing and when you have everything. The devil knows this and it's important that we know it too. We must remember to stay close to God in both the good times and the bad times. Whether you are in a season when things are going good or a season when nothing is going right, God has promised to supply all of your needs according to His riches in glory as you seek Him first and honor Him with your finances. If you are going through a lack attack, keep your eyes fixed on the Lord, the One who loves you. He will never leave you or forsake you.

STAND FIRM IN PRAYER

As believers we need to learn to stand firm in prayer. There is no "gift of prayer," but rather, prayer is a discipline that takes action on our part. It takes faith and persistence to live a life of prayer, however, there are times when even though you are faithful to pray,

Inhale - God's word
exhale - prayer

What to do when your mind is clouded while praying.

your mind may work against you. It's not only the normal or natural duties and cares of life that keep you from your place of prayer and time of prayer; it is an unseen spiritual tactic of the devil to choke prayer out of your life.

Often when I try to pray and focus my thoughts on the Lord, I realize my thoughts are on everything *but* God. In my mind I'm going over the hundreds of things I need to do instead of focusing on prayer. I've learned to fight against this by taking a pen and small notepad and writing down all the things I've forgotten to do. Then I take my list and say, "Thank you, devil, for reminding me of all these things, and now that they are out of the way, I'm going to pray!"

The key to a strong and healthy spiritual life is to inhale the word of God by reading your Bible, and exhaling with prayer. The Bible is the inspired Word of God, which means it is "God-breathed." When you read the Bible, you "breathe in" your spiritual life, and when you pray, you breathe out the Spirit of God into the world around you. To stay healthy physically we must breathe in and breathe out, and so it is with our spiritual lives also.

In every failure of my life there have always been two common denominators: a dusty Bible and a broken-down altar. If you are not reading your Bible on a regular basis and praying, you are under spiritual attack.

Learn how to recognize when your prayer life is under attack, and ask the Holy Spirit for strategies to keep you breathing in and exhaling God's life-giving breath.

Take Every Thought Captive to Christ

Sometimes it seems everywhere you turn there is another problem, and another problem, and another problem. With problems lined up as far as the eye can see, you begin to feel like there is no escape. Thoughts such as, "What's the use? Why even try? Nothing is changing," begin to flood your mind and frustration takes hold. I read somewhere that frustration is fear that your efforts will not pay off. If you are feeling overwhelmed by circumstances, more than likely the devil is involved.

The word *circumstance* comes from two words: *circum* (encircle) and *stance* (stand). When you are feeling overwhelmed by circumstances, you are standing encircled by what's going on while the devil plants seeds of a bad attitude. He wants to get you to that place of hopelessness, where you just feel like giving up. Proverbs 13:12 says, "Hope deferred makes the heart sick" (MEV). Satan wants to defer your hope to the point of hopelessness.

I want you to understand something about hopelessness. It does not come on all at once. When you hit that wall and just feel like throwing in the towel and quitting, know that thought formed in your spirit long before. But we are more than conquerors in Christ Jesus! We do not have to give in to the devil's schemes. We can fight on the battleground of the mind by taking every thought captive to Christ (2 Cor. 10:5). Quitting should never be an option for a believer.

If quitting is *never* an option, then when difficult times hit you, instead of giving in to hopelessness, you keep pressing on in faith that God's strength is greater than yours and He will see you through every battle. The writer of Hebrews says, "Faith is the substance of things hoped for, the evidence of things not seen" (Heb. 11:1, MEV). Learn to cultivate the faith to see what is not yet, even in the midst of your most difficult circumstances, and God will see you through.

EMBRACE THE TRUTH THAT COMES FROM THE HOLY SPIRIT

When old iniquities begin to resurface in your life, and you start letting go of godly relationships, you had better believe Satan is at the root of the issue. But just what is an iniquity? Some consider iniquities to be those old habits that your soul wants to fall back on when things don't seem to be going your way—things such as smoking, drug abuse, excessive drinking, visiting the bars or clubs, indulging the flesh.

Iniquities also have to do with wickedness and injustice, such as lying, cheating, and stealing from others. They include sexual sins such as fornication (sleeping with people to whom you are not married), pornography, and adultery. Often this type of attack begins with a longing for your former lifestyle. Perhaps you have thought, "Well, at least when I was in the world, I had this or did that."

Like the Israelites complaining in the wilderness, you have selective memory if you are thinking this way. When Moses led the people of Israel out of Egyptian slavery, every time they encountered a little hardship they complained and wanted to go back—*to slavery!* After a miraculous deliverance out of Egypt, across the Red Sea, and into safety, they got a little hungry and the complaints started rolling out again. "Oh, that we had died by the hand of the LORD in the land of Egypt, when we sat by the pots of meat and when we ate bread to the full! For you have brought us out into this wilderness to kill this whole assembly with hunger" (Exod. 16:3, NKJV).

As children of God, we can fall into the same patterns of thinking when we find ourselves "in the wilderness" of life. If you find yourself going back to old iniquities that God has set you free from, or even just thinking about these things, it is time to pay attention to the warning conviction of the Holy Spirit.

When old iniquities start tempting you, the next sign of spiritual attack is typically to pull away from godly relationships. Your friends provide a snapshot of your life now and in the future. Take a moment to take stock of your relationships. Have you pulled out of relationships with people at church or with people in your small group? Are more and more of your friends carnally minded rather than spiritually minded? If that's you, make no mistake, you are stumbling around the battleground and the enemy has a target drawn on your head.

Don't be afraid to be identified as a believer. Embrace the truth of the Holy Spirit in your life and learn to live from a place of peace even in those wilderness times. When your life is full of God and filled with His Spirit, your unsaved friends will be drawn to you because they will see Christ in you. Live proactively, allowing God to bring His kingdom to earth through you.

> Our Father in heaven, hallowed be your name, your kingdom come, *your will be done,* on earth as it is in heaven.
> —MATTHEW 6:9–10, NIV, EMPHASIS ADDED

Chapter Three

THE "DO NOTS" OF THE KINGDOM

THE DEVIL PROWLS around like a lion, ready to pounce on believers, and for that reason you must learn how to "arm" yourself so you can deal effectively with that lion when he comes to stalk you. I have five "Do Nots" that I carry around in my quiver to help me push back an attack of the enemy, and I want to share them with you because they work!

Do not forget who made you.

God created you with the storms of life in mind. In fact, He designed you to be weatherproof. You can let the winds blow and the storms rage around you because you are going to make it through with Christ who lives in you. You are God's child. He loves you and cares about you, and He wants to see you succeed.

I've watched footage of hurricanes as they move onto land. The winds of a hurricane can break massive oak trees like matchsticks, but not palm trees because palm trees are designed to bend but not break. The Bible says the righteous will flourish like a palm tree (Ps. 92:12). God has designed you to withstand the attacks of the enemy. The storms of your life may bend you, but they can't break you. They may drive you to your knees, but on your knees is a good place to find Jesus.

God built you with storms in mind and He has given you bounce-back power. He has put a bounce in you like a rubber ball. If life has you down, remember: the harder you fall, the higher you bounce back. Micah 7:8 says, "Do not rejoice over me, my enemy; when I fall, I will arise" (NKJV)

Do not forsake the time and place of prayer.

I've learned that there are two things that are vital to a successful prayer life: a *time of prayer* and a *place of prayer*. There's a real dynamic that begins to take place when you pray consistently in the same place for years—praying, worshipping, and thanking God for His goodness in the times when everything is going great, and also praying through the tough times when the tears are flowing and the burdens and trials of life feel overwhelming. When you are going through hardships, when you are fighting battles, when it feels as if all hell is fighting against you—it can be hard to pray. Having an established time and place of prayer will help you in the midst of battle.

For me the right time is in the morning, and the right place is the beautiful country trails in the woods near my home that I've been walking daily for decades. I've prayed and walked along these trails through all four seasons—in the spring as the plant life blooms, in the summer when the leaves are bright and green, when they are colorful in the fall, and in the winter when many have fallen. Sometimes I'm just in shorts, a shirt, and sneakers; at other times I'm wearing gloves, a heavy coat, and a hat. But no matter the season, when I walk those trails in the morning I say, "God, I am here to be with You."

Your place of prayer may be a room in your house, a quiet field, a spot in the woods. It can be any place that you have consecrated to God as your meeting place with Him. Without a place of prayer, you will be less and less likely to meet with Him on a consistent basis. Even when you don't know what to pray, if you just go to your place of prayer, you can let God do the talking. Just going to your place of prayer is an act of surrender to His will for your life. Your physical presence there says, "I want to hear from You, Father. I don't know what to say, what to pray, but I am here." Oftentimes I will go to my place of prayer and just wait on God, and He always shows up.

Do not forsake the place of power.

The devil is always looking to maneuver you out of a place of God's power and into a weak and vulnerable position. When you get into a spiritual battle, the enemy will try to pull you away from church, because church is a place of power. When you get up on a Sunday morning and the devil starts giving you all sorts of reasons why you should stay home from church, that's when you should rustle around and make sure you get out that door and into church. As long as the prodigal son was in the father's house, he was safe; it was when he abandoned the father's house and went into a foreign country that he lost everything.

In Psalm 20 the people prayed for David, "May the LORD answer you in the day of trouble; may the name of the God of Jacob defend you; *may He send you help from the sanctuary,* and strengthen you from Zion" (vv. 1–2, MEV, emphasis added). Don't let Satan make you forsake the place of power. And don't be a tumbleweed, blowing from church to church, rootless and fruitless. Become a mighty oak of righteousness, planted by streams of living water, God's living water!

Do not forsake the power of partnership.

God wants us to use wisdom in choosing which relationships to cultivate. You don't need to support toxic, dysfunctional, draining relationships. You need the power of partnership that holy relationships provide. It is good to be around people who have lived longer and done more than you have. You can glean from their experience, including their mistakes. Remember, "Iron sharpens iron" (Prov. 27:17, MEV).

The enemy's tactics never change. He wants to divide and conquer. That is how the snake Satan first deceived Eve; he got her alone and twisted the words of God. Wise Solomon said, "Two are better than one, because they have a good reward for their labor. For if they fall, one will lift up his companion. But woe to him who is alone when he falls, for he has no one to help him up" (Eccles. 4:9–10, NKJV). When you are going through an attack, you don't need dead-beat friends who want to drag you down further. You need to be around spiritual giants who have fought the good fight of faith and are still standing. Treasure those relationships and the power of partnership God brings into your life.

Do not disconnect from pastoral protection.

I have often seen people under attack whom I wanted to pull close and help, but they refused. Do not wait until your enemy is tearing you to pieces to seek the aid of those in a pastoral role in your life. God has given pastors the responsibility of feeding and protecting the flock. That is why Hebrews 13:17 says, "Obey those who rule over you, and be submissive, for they watch out for your souls, as those who must give account. Let them do so with joy and not with grief, for that would be unprofitable for you" (NKJV).

A shepherd's staff has a hook on the end used for pulling a lamb out of danger. His rod is used as a weapon against predators. David said of the Lord, the Good Shepherd, "Yea, though I walk through the valley of the shadow of death, I will fear no evil; for You are with me; Your rod and Your staff, they comfort me" (Ps. 23:4, NKJV). Allow your pastor to protect you and shepherd you through the snares of life. God has tasked pastors with the job of tending their sheep because He knows we will need tending! The shepherd can see the wolf coming even when you don't know you are under attack.

God Is Faithful

I remember a season in my life when I went through a lot of challenges. There were days when it felt like I was in the darkest valley of my ministry, and I just couldn't take anymore. I knew I was under attack and so I took a walk in the woods to pray. Eventually I came to a massive oak tree where I had often prayed before. As I stood there meditating and praying, crying out to God, I found myself picking up a rock and carving a mark into that massive old tree.

"God," I cried out. "Do You see this mark right here? I don't understand everything that I'm going through right now. I don't know why it is happening. But I do know that you will give me victory in this fight, and the mark on this tree will be a lasting reminder."

Then I said, "Satan, I want you to see this mark too, because I'm never going to give up. I am not going down without a fight. I am never going to stop. I am going to keep going after God harder than ever because this attack must mean that you sense something good is about to break loose in my life."

Since that day I have had many opportunities to look at that mark and confidently reflect on how God brought me through and gave me the victory in that situation. It reminds me that God is faithful, and He *will* do it again.

Is it time to mark a tree in your life? Are you in the midst of a spiritual attack and just can't imagine how you will overcome? Sometimes the battles we face last for days, or months, or even years. They try our sanity. That's when you must take hold of the promises of God and stand strong in the faith, putting on the whole armor of God, with confidence that He is with you.

You may not have a literal tree to mark as I did, but you can go to your prayer place, put on God's armor, and fill up on the Word of God. If you will take a stand, God will show up. He will make a message out of your mess. Trust Him, and you will walk away with a testimony of victory.

Chapter Four

KNOW YOUR ENEMY

SCRIPTURE TELLS US that spiritual battles are taking place all around us because we live in two atmospheres at the same time. One is a physical atmosphere that we can see, smell, hear, touch, and taste. The other is a spiritual atmosphere that we cannot see with our natural eye or experience with the rest of our natural senses, but which is very real. The devil knows the power of atmosphere, and as believers, we need to know it as well. Whenever possible, Satan will try and tempt you into the wrong atmosphere in order to make it easier for you to fall into sin. Think about it—would you be more likely to fall into sinful behavior in a library or in a wild club or party scene? The answer is pretty obvious because it's the atmosphere that makes the difference. Put another way, you can grow bananas in Jamaica but not in Alaska. Why? The atmosphere is right for banana growing in Jamaica, but it's not right in Alaska. There's something about the atmosphere of a club—the lights, the music, the dancing—it creates an environment that is right for sin. The atmosphere creates a climate, and the climate creates a culture. If the enemy can get you in *his* culture, he knows he can get you to sin.

God understands the power of atmosphere as well. He is everywhere—but He does not manifest His presence equally everywhere. He will manifest His presence when the atmosphere is right, and he loves an atmosphere of praise and of true worship from His people. He loves a celebration! The Bible says that God inhabits the praises of His people (Ps. 22:3). The word *inhabits* means that God is enthroned (feels comfortable enough to sit down) in the place where the atmosphere is filled with celebration, praise, and worship. When you fill the atmosphere with complaining, fault-finding, and murmuring, it's not inviting to the presence of God. In fact, it does just the opposite.

The same is true with the Holy Spirit: atmosphere is everything. The atmosphere of holiness, purity, praise, worship, prayer, love, and unity attract the Holy Spirit—just as an atmosphere of lust, drunkenness, anger, and hatred attracts demonic spirits. If you are filled with the Holy Spirit, and He is dominating your life, then the fruit of the Spirit—love, joy, peace, long-suffering, kindness, goodness, faithfulness, self-control, and gentleness—will become increasingly evident in your life (Gal. 5:22–23). When the fruit of the Spirit is in your life, you naturally create an atmosphere for the presence of the Holy Spirit. "And in him you too are being built together to become a dwelling in which God lives by his Spirit" (Eph. 2:22, NIV). As you respond to the presence of God, He releases greater measures of His presence.

Often people will receive healing or supernatural deliverance from addictions during a powerful worship service, or before an altar call is ever given, because the atmosphere is charged with the presence of God. Unsaved people will get out of their seats, weeping, and walk to the front to repent and ask Jesus into their lives when they encounter His presence. In this kind of an environment, with such holiness present, sinners simply can't stand their sin any longer. Under the conviction of the Holy Spirit they are compelled to come forward. And when people begin to respond to the presence of God, He responds in greater measure. That's the kind of atmosphere I love to be in!

Fight Spirit With Spirit

We are at war, but we cannot fight in the spirit realm with our natural ability, nor with our education, our money, or our natural resources. We can only fight spirit with spirit, "For the weapons of our warfare are not carnal but mighty in God for pulling down strongholds" (2 Cor. 10:4, NKJV).

Demonic spirits with different ranks and assignments

exist in the spiritual realm, and they respond to atmospheres. All spirits seek expression of their will into time and space, but they cannot accomplish this without someone providing them the opportunity. If a demonic spirit manifests, it is because somebody allowed it and created an atmosphere for that spirit to operate.

When the disciples asked Jesus why they were unable to cast the evil spirit out of the child, Jesus said, "This kind does not go out except by prayer and fasting" (Matt. 17:21, NKJV). "This kind" would indicate that there are spirits with different ranks. Without going into an expository work on demonology, let's briefly examine a few of the different types of evil spirits mentioned in the Bible.

Tormenting or vexing spirits

A tormenting or vexing spirit is a lower-ranking demon that comes to oppose your mind and bring depression, fear, and excessive worry. Having a bad day is not necessarily an indication that you are being tormented by a demon—real life can be difficult. But when you feel oppressed all the time, so much so that your mind and emotions are in turmoil—you feel down, depressed, discouraged, and hopeless—that is a tormenting spirit.

When a tormenting spirit gets hold of your mind,

thoughts such as harming yourself or even suicide* can take hold as the enemy whispers suggestions to you. When a vexing spirit tries to torment you, your first response should be to take authority over it and rebuke it in the name of Jesus. Do not give in to those negative, harmful, demonic thoughts of despair. Resist them. If you humble yourself and resist the devil, he *will* flee.

We must never doubt that as born-again believers we have been given authority over any demon that tries to torment our lives. God gives us "the garment of praise" for the spirit of heaviness or despair (Isa. 61:3, MEV). As a Christian, the greatest thing you can do to combat depression and oppression in your mind is to put on the garment of praise. Put on some worship music and transform your heart and mind into an attitude of gratitude, think on good things and watch your praise change the atmosphere and cause a shift in the spiritual realm.

Learn to speak "praise phrases" to defeat tormenting spirits of the mind. Verbally praise the Lord, saying things such as, "You are good! You are working all things together for my good." Don't give in and begin to say words that make the devil think he's winning. Atmosphere is everything. Speak words of praise, and that spirit of heaviness will lift.

---

* If you have thoughts of harming yourself or others, it's imperative that you seek professional help in addition to following the advice provided in this book.

Deceiving spirits

Paul told Timothy, "Now the Spirit expressly says that in latter times some will depart from the faith, *giving heed to deceiving spirits and doctrines of demons*" (1 Tim. 4:1, NKJV, emphasis added). Paul is telling us that there are demons that pervert teachings; who twist the Word of God, and lead people away from the faith. They are called deceiving spirits. Such deceiving spirits will always put forth wrong teaching, false teaching, and wrong thought patterns.

Any time you open yourself up to doctrines of demons and false teachings—including horoscopes, fortune-tellers, palm readers, and psychics—you are opening the door to Satan's plan for your life. When you do this, you are getting yourself into spiritual territory that you cannot conquer on your own. Any believer can take authority over a vexing spirit, but only pastors, teachers, evangelists, prophets, and apostles have authority to take the Word of God and teach truth against doctrines of devils and false teachings. If you or someone you know has opened the door to deceiving spirits, I encourage you to seek the counsel of your pastor or a mature believer in Christ.

Territorial spirits

Territorial spirits are higher-level territorial principalities that try to exert control over certain geographical areas. Cities such as Las Vegas with gambling, Los

Angeles with entertainment, New York with finance, and Washington DC with politics and power have territorial spirits—demonic powers trying to control their geographical area. Territorial spirits want to control the culture over cities, regions, states, and nations.

It takes a community of believers praying and fasting and establishing strong churches in those cities, regions, and states to deal with the territorial principalities assaulting them in high places. Jesus said, "I will build My church, and the gates of Hades [hell] shall not prevail against it" (Matt. 16:18, MEV). That is what Paul was talking about when he said, "His intent was that now, *through the church*, the manifold wisdom of God should be made known to the rulers and authorities in the heavenly realms" (Eph. 3:10, NIV, emphasis added).

Take Authority Over Demons

As believers we have been given authority over demons. The only way demons can get a stranglehold of us is when we deliberately and persistently walk in sin. If a believer encounters what he thinks is a true manifestation of demon oppression or possession, he has the authority and the power of the Holy Spirit to expel that demon power.

If you or someone you know does encounter a person you suspect is demon possessed, you should call upon a trusted mature believer to aid you, and gather at least two or three together to pray for guidance in the situation. There are certain signs of demonic possession to look for when trying to determine if a demon is at work in someone.

A sure sign of demonic possession is someone empowered with incredible strength. Demons will often energize people in this way. An example of this is found in Scripture, in the story of the Gadarene demoniac in Mark 5. This man had been bound with heavy chains and broke them; no one could subdue him due to the demonic strength operating in him. I have seen a few people who were demon possessed, and it sometimes took five or six people to subdue them due to the superhuman strength that possessed them.

A person who is demon possessed may have spontaneous reactions of uncontrolled cursing when the name of Jesus Christ is spoken. This uncontrolled compulsion to blaspheme the name of God can be a sign of demonic influence, as can a radical change in personality.

An evil spirit can cause contortions in facial features and countenance. A person's eyes can become glazed and even roll back in their head. Their look and even their voice will change. When someone is set free, they will usually come immediately back into their "right mind." Their voice will normalize, and you will see a total change in their demeanor.

As I mentioned previously when discussing tormenting and vexing spirits, deep depression, despondency, and suicidal tendencies can also be signs of demonic attack. These conditions can go beyond spiritual torment to a level that we would consider demonic possession or oppression.*

There are some examples in Scripture of demon-possessed people who tried to harm themselves. After Satan used Judas for his purpose, he then used the power of guilt to drive Judas to self-destruction. You will recall that Judas went out and hanged himself when he realized what he had done. The demon-possessed boy in Matthew 17:14–15 had a strong tendency for self-destruction. He would throw himself into the fire and then into the water as the demon tried to inflict harm and self-destruction on him. The Gadarene demoniac gashed himself with sharp stones, indicating how demons arouse a tendency toward self-destruction.

We see this same type of self-destructive behavior today in teenage girls who cut themselves. Cutting does not necessarily indicate demon possession, but certainly the voice telling them to slash themselves or starve themselves with anorexia is not the voice

---

* Be careful when weighing any of these symptoms, which can be brought on by other causes such as chemical imbalances or mental illnesses. Seek professional help if you or someone you are trying to help experiences thoughts of self-harm or harming others.

of the Holy Spirit. It is important to understand that every case of suicide or of self-destructive behavior is different, but when a person repeatedly tries to harm himself or herself, there is a strong possibility that person could be under demonic attack.

Extreme caution should be used when discerning whether or not someone is demon possessed. In my more than twenty-five years of ministry I have encountered only five people whom I was convinced needed some form of exorcism. It is my experience that, when attempting to cast out demons, it should almost always be done in a private setting with a pastor or other mature, balanced spiritual leaders present.

The position of every born-again believer should reflect James 4:7, which says, "Resist the devil, and he will flee from you" (MEV). Jesus Christ in His ultimate commission to the church said, "In My name they will cast out demons" (Mark 16:17, MEV). While we should always seek the help of a mature Christian leader when dealing with challenging ministry situations, we should not be afraid to take authority over demons as a believer in Jesus Christ.

There is a passage of Scripture in the Book of Isaiah that gives us a key to the origin of evil.

> How art thou fallen from heaven, O Lucifer, son
> of the morning! How art thou cut down to the
> ground, which didst weaken the nations! For

thou hast said in thine heart, I will ascend into heaven, I will exalt my throne above the stars of God: I will sit also upon the mount of the congregation, in the sides of the north: I will ascend above the heights of the clouds; I will be like the most High.

—Isaiah 14:12–14, kjv

Here we find God mourning over this creature He had created and loved. This creature is the one we call Satan, first described as *Lucifer*, which means "the shining one." Lucifer was so beautiful he would literally shine with the glory of God while he was still in heaven.

It is verse 13 that gives us the real description of evil, "For thou has said in thine heart. . . ." That's where evil always begins—in the heart. Lucifer filled his heart with rebellion. He chose to act independently of God because he thought himself so magnificent, so beautiful, so filled with power, that he should have some of the worship of the universe for himself. "I will ascend to heaven," he said. "I will be like the most High." Lucifer wanted to be God. He wanted to be in charge. He wanted the glory.

We are told in Revelation 12 that one-third of the angelic realm followed Lucifer in his revolt. I don't believe Lucifer lost any of his great intellect, beauty, or power when he rebelled and became the first sinful creature. I believe he used these traits to entice many angels to join his ranks. But he did lose the one thing that would make him function correctly: a personal relationship with God. At that moment of Lucifer's rebellion, God's perfect universe became impure. The pollution of sin entered the earth when Satan and his angels revolted.

Today we know Lucifer by many names—Satan, the devil, the evil one, the accuser, the adversary. Beautiful little planet Earth has become the arena of the mightiest contest of all time—a contest between good and evil, a contest between God and Satan, a contest where God Himself would be wounded in a life-and-death struggle with the powers of darkness, because in the garden God gave the title deed of the world to Satan, and since then the world has been under his control.

The Bible gives Satan three titles that describe his work. First, he is called "the ruler of this world" (John 12:31, MEV), which means he is constantly at work in government and political systems in nations throughout the world. Satan's second title is "prince of the power of the air." Ephesians 2:1–2 says, "And you were dead in your trespasses and sins, in which you formerly walked according to the age of this world and according to the prince of the power of the air, the spirit who now works in the sons of disobedience" (MEV). The word translated as "air" in this scripture literally means "the air we breathe," and it is speaking of "mood" or "atmosphere of thought." We often use the term *atmosphere* in this sense. For instance, if someone says, "Paris has a romantic atmosphere," you would understand that they were talking about a certain mood or feeling in the air.

In his letter to the Ephesians, Paul calls Satan the prince of the "atmosphere of thoughts." In this role Satan injects his brainwashing into the educational system, mass media, arts, and culture. His deceptions about life and its purpose are lethal.

Before you believe in Jesus Christ, you are unwittingly dominated by Satan's atmosphere of thought. When the Holy Spirit enlightens your mind to realize that Satan is the ruler over all these thought forms, and to understand how he bombards you every day by these sources, you begin to see how deadly the prince of the power of the air can be. It is for this reason we must focus our hearts on Jesus and constantly allow our minds to be renewed with God's view of life, which is alien from the human viewpoint of the world's systems. Romans 12:2 says, "And do not be conformed to this world, but be transformed by the renewing of your mind" (NKJV).

The third title of Satan is "the god of this age" (2 Cor. 4:4, NKJV), which means the prevailing thought of a particular era. The god of this age refers to Satan's activity in relation to Christianity.

BRING EVERYTHING TO THE LIGHT

Satan and his demons prefer to do their work without being exposed. They definitely don't like to be identified and cast out. Demons will resist exposure and will resist anyone who attempts to bring the light of God upon their hidden works. Once the enemy has gained ground and set up the kind of culture he desires, he wants us to buzz off and to leave him be. Some ministries unconsciously fall into the trap of the enemy by *leaving him alone*. Luke 4:33–34 tells us that while ministering in Capernaum, Jesus encountered a man in the synagogue with a demon who cried out in a loud voice, "Let us alone!" (NKJV).

Ministers of the gospel who don't want to deal with the subject of demons often say that all they need to do is preach Jesus. I'm certainly not against preaching Jesus, but I also find in Luke 4:18 that we are called to preach deliverance to the captives. Jesus was a deliverance preacher. In Mark 6:13 He cast out many demons. Today most ministries—including mine—cast out few if any demons. Many don't want to deal with this aspect of the ministry of our Lord. Well-meaning Christians, pastors included, feel it unnecessary to discuss or teach on spiritual warfare, and are quick to label anyone who does spend time studying and teaching in these areas of Scripture "overboard," "radical," or a "demon-chaser." But we must make no mistake—avoidance of spiritual warfare teaching is just what the enemy wants. The less you discuss and attack his kingdom, the more he will be able to operate under the cover of darkness.

When demons were exposed in Jesus's day they screamed, cursed, and cried out. They will try and do the same today, but that is no reason to avoid them. In fact, you can command them to be quiet, in Jesus's name. If demons are left alone, they will continue to operate unhindered in the lives of countless individuals, and that's precisely why they cannot and should not be left alone. We must expose them and cast them out by the power of God's Word and the Holy Spirit.

According to Ephesians 6:12 demons are identified as "the rulers of the darkness of this world" (MEV). A demon's level of authority to operate is based upon the darkness in a person's life. The more darkness, the more authority they have. In contrast, when revelation from God's Word concerning the devil's works and schemes comes into a person's mind, then light comes. And when light comes, the darkness is dispelled and along with it, the rulers of the darkness. Their power is broken by the power of God's light. That is why Satan and his demons would rather be left alone in the dark.

In Exodus 14:12 the Hebrews said the same thing to Moses that the demons said to Jesus: "*Let us alone* that we may serve the Egyptians" (MEV, emphasis added). They were being motivated by the spirits of bondage, slavery, and fear, which came from the devil.

Mark 6:13 says that Jesus and His disciples "cast out many devils" (KJV). Why did they do that? Because they, the demons, were there! Part of Jesus's mandate was to expose the powers of darkness and set the captives free. And that mandate has been passed on to us. The Lord is raising up ministries that will not leave demons alone, but will expose and defeat them with the power and light of God's truth. We are called to challenge, confront, and expose the works of darkness. "But through knowledge the righteous will be delivered" (Prov. 11:9, NKJV).

The religious system of Jesus's day would not disturb Satan and his demons. Instead, they coexisted with them. Everything was humming right along in the darkness until Jesus entered the temple and cast out those who were in cahoots with the devil. He infuriated and exposed Satan and his demons by teaching and preaching the truth of God's Word. Jesus knew that you can't cast the devil out if you're best friends with him.

CREATE A CLIMATE OF GOD'S PRESENCE

The enemy is out to set up a culture that is void of the power of God. Even in the church there is little difference between some Christians' lifestyles and the world's lifestyles. The morals are very much alike and reflective of one another. Satan is able to set up his culture when we respond to any of the spiritual influences or activities I've just described, because we have created an atmosphere that enables the devil. We can counter Satan's atmosphere by creating a climate for the presence of God.

The atmosphere you sustain over time will create a climate, which I also call a predictable pattern. For example, you might live in an area that has a hot day now and then, but that does not create a hot climate. A hot climate is what you would experience in a tropical area where temperatures are always balmy. A *climate* is created when the same thing is repeated over and over.

Whenever we sustain a spiritual atmosphere of sin and iniquity, a demonic climate takes shape. Conversely whenever we sustain a spiritual atmosphere of praise and thankfulness, a climate of God's presence begins to form. If a sustained atmosphere creates a climate, then it follows that a climate creates a stronghold. It is the stronghold that defines the culture of a place. Demonic spirits fight for control in order to control the culture of our lives and even of nations, and set up strongholds.

IMPOSE THE AUTHORITY OF THE KINGDOM

I have heard it said that Christians are not to be spiritual *thermometers* but spiritual *thermostats*. In other words, we are not merely supposed to *detect* the spiritual climate as a thermometer detects the existing temperature in a room; we are to *change* the spiritual climate, imposing the authority of the kingdom of God wherever we go! It is important to understand atmospheres and our ability to change them because Jesus has authorized and empowered us in this arena.

Jesus changed the atmosphere in His region, and we have the power to change the atmosphere and usher the presence and power of God into our situations, our homes, and our churches. This is how we keep the devil out—by imposing the authority of the kingdom of God on him.

Keep a spirit of prayer and praise in your life and it will create the right atmosphere around you. When you have unsaved loved ones who need to hear the message of the gospel but something keeps blocking them from hearing and receiving, do not back down. Instead, change the atmosphere with prayer and praise, stand and fight, filled with the Holy Spirit. Go to the throne of grace on your knees and intercede for them. God will meet you and partner with you to bring His kingdom to bear on the kingdoms of this world.

Souls are at stake. People we love are bound in sin, and many still stumble in darkness. But we have a remedy and His name is Jesus. He has given us the authority to stand between new converts, between our families, our children and the spirit of this age that wants to pervert the truth of God and turn everyone away from the light. We are to fast, pray, praise, worship, intercede, stand, and wage war in the spiritual realm, so that our enemy, the devil, cannot work his way into our lives and squeeze the life out of us, rendering us ineffective for God. Don't allow yourself to grow weary in doing the work of the kingdom. Remember the words of Revelation 11:15: "Then the seventh angel sounded; and there were loud voices in heaven, saying, 'The kingdom of the world has become the kingdom of our Lord and of His Christ; and He will reign forever and ever'" (NAS).

Chapter Five

CROSS OVER

T oo many Christians today worship God from afar. We go to church on Sunday morning, barely raise our hands, and when it's all over, we leave God at the back door and go do whatever we want to do the rest of the week. We give Him superficial worship from a distance, not wanting to get too close.

Jesus encountered this same type of behavior in His ministry. In Mark chapter 5 we find the story of the Gadarene demoniac. We are told that Jesus was on His way to the land of the Gadarenes. I have seen this land. It is a territory on the east side of the Sea of Galilee and the Jordan River. Now the Gadarenes have an interesting history, which dates back to the twelve tribes of Israel. They were descendants of the tribe of Gad. You might recall that when Joshua led the children of Israel across the Jordan River into the Promised Land, the tribe of Gad, along with Reuben and half of Manasseh, did not cross over with them.

The tribe of Gad received Moses's permission to

establish cities and settle permanently along the east side of the Jordan, if their men would help the Israelites conquer the land when they first crossed over. Finding the land on the east side of the river good for their livestock, they wanted to keep their children protected from the Canaanites on the other side of the Jordan, so they struck up a compromise. Just like that, they gave up their inheritance.

To my way of thinking, they represent what I call "borderline Christians." Rather than trusting God to lead them safely into unknown territory, they were willing to trust what they could see with their own eyes. They followed God to a certain point and then they simply stopped trusting Him. They weren't even remotely interested in going and possessing everything God said they could have. Instead, they were content to camp out on the borderline while the rest of God's people followed Him into their destiny.

The people of Gad remained on the border as God's presence moved farther and farther away. By the time the ark of the covenant resided in Jerusalem, they were one of the tribes farthest away from the presence of God. Remember, the ark of the covenant was the "throne zone," the place where the presence of God resided. When the Israelites crossed the Jordan and took the Promised Land, they carried the ark of God's presence out before them.

Some Christians today are like the tribe of Gad. We get saved, but when we reach the very edge of God's promise, we are willing to pitch our tents and make compromises. We're willing to camp out on the borderline of God's presence rather than trusting Him to take us forward into the Promised Land.

Does this sound like you? Have you decided to trust your own wisdom instead of trusting God? Are you willing to settle for what you can see with your own eyes instead of trusting God to take you through to His promised land? Are you camped out on the borderline, unaware of how far you really are from God's presence?

There is a reason people don't want to come close to God, into the place of worship. Because when you really get close to the presence of God, you begin to act like He acts and live like He lives. You begin to take on His nature, His character, and His appetites. You can't get close to the presence of God and live like *you* want to live and do what *you* want to do. Instead of "crossing the Jordan," we develop a way of avoiding intimacy with God. We have a form of godliness, but we deny its power. We have these little yuppie, high-tech churches now. We just come in and do a little this and do a little that and then go live any way we want to. But the truth is, you can't keep doing what you want to and get close to God at the same time. You can't set up camp on the borderline and never follow Him into the deeper things He has for you. There comes a point when you have to walk it and live it, or you're simply not in relationship with Him.

I find it interesting that Jesus included the land of the Gadarenes in His itinerary. I doubt He was going there just to deliver a demon-possessed man. I believe He had a historical account to settle in that city, because these people had gotten so far from the presence of God. Under the law Jews were forbidden to raise pigs and yet that is exactly what the Gadarenes were doing. By Jewish law they could not even touch a pig, let alone eat one, because pigs were considered filthy and unclean. But there they were, living so far from the presence of God that they forgot how He told them to live.

They gave in to the temptation to settle on the borderline because of what they could see with their own eyes. Instead of looking to God as their source, they were looking all around them and taking matters into their own hands, trusting their own decisions. It's amazing what you'll get involved in when you get away from God's presence. You think it's OK to live your life your way, and the next thing you know, you're raising pigs! The very thing God said has no place in your life, that's the thing you're now using as your main source of income.

I believe Jesus was on His way to the land of Gadarenes because He intended to clean them up. Notice that as soon as He stepped off the boat, He was confronted by a demon-possessed man. I think this man was a reflection of what the Gadarenes had become. When an individual or a church or a nation pulls away from the presence of God, demons start taking over. Intense demonic activity will set itself up when we draw back from the presence of God and the place of worship. While this is true, the good news is that the opposite is also true—when we draw near to God, He will draw near to us. His presence will push out the dark and replace it with His marvelous light!

Refuse to Compromise Evil

Have you noticed how we live in a society that has a fascination with the dead and the occult? While we call psychic hotlines and watch *Celebrity Ghost Stories* on TV, our kids entertain themselves with movies and books about vampires such as *Twilight* and with TV shows about zombies such as *The Walking Dead*. Just like the people of Gad let the pigs into their lives, we've allowed the devil into our lives, giving him access through the entertainment industry and the Internet. Our children are downloading and listening to Satanic music, and we shrug and say such things as, "Oh, it's not that bad." When we get too comfortable with the devil, we end up befriending him. He just creeps into our lives, and we move over and make room for him.

There's an old story that illustrates this well. A man found a wounded snake on the road, and having compassion, he took it home and nursed it back to health. After spending so much time with the snake, he didn't feel any danger when he was around it. In fact, he had grown quite fond of it and practically considered it a pet. Then one day, as he was feeding the snake, it bit him on the hand and its poisonous venom quickly spread throughout his body. As he lay there dying, he looked at the snake with complete disbelief in his eyes. "I took such good care of you, I fed you and kept you safe. How could you bite me?" he said. Without the slightest bit of remorse the snake sneered as it hissed in reply. "S-s-s-silly man. *You knew I was a snake when you took me in.*"

What pigs have you let into your parlor? What sins have you in your life that you are convinced are harmless? Sin may seem like fun for a season, but eventually it will lead you straight off a cliff. When you know something is a sin, walk away! Don't open the door and let the devil slither into your life. You may think you can control sin, but you can't. The demon-possessed man in Gadarene was uncontrollable. He had a violent spirit of rage that terrorized everyone around him. He was bound with chains but could not be restrained. We can't just wiggle our noses like Samantha on *Bewitched* and expect the demons to disappear. TV is fantasy, but the devil is real.

The devil is very real and very busy terrorizing our world today. We see him when men beat their wives, when pedophiles prey on children, in the world of human trafficking, when gang members kill, when someone goes on a shooting rampage in a theatre, or a church. Satan is all around us, but he and his demons know who Jesus is, and the authority He carries. When Jesus stepped out of that boat in Gadarene, the Bible says the demons "saw Jesus from afar" (Mark 5:6, MEV). They recognized Him instantly and were terrified because they knew who He was; they knew the authority He carried.

When we walk into a room, the devil ought to get uncomfortable because of Christ in us. Demons ought to get upset when a man or woman full of the Holy Ghost walks into their territory. Some of you wonder why you get attacked so much. You just go into a store, minding your own business, paying for some gas, and some guy turns around and says, "Blankity, blank, blank, blank!" He is reacting like that to you because the Holy Spirit in you is upsetting the unclean spirits all around you. Don't be upset when this happens. The Holy Ghost is just doing his thing—He is on a mission to terrorize the devil. Christ in you will force evil to compromise. That's who we are as a people of God. Evil must obey the Christ in us rather than us compromising evil.

In Mark 5:9–15 Jesus asks, "What is your name," and the demons answer, "My name is Legion, for we are many" (NKJV). *Legion* is a military word that was used to describe a Roman unit of soldiers that would contain a minimum of six thousand to ten thousand soldiers. Notice that the next thing the demons said was, "We know you're going to throw us out. But please give us a place to go." I love that! You see, one thing you need to understand about demons is that when they come into the presence of Jesus, they don't do what they want to do anymore. They don't go where they want to go. When a demon gets in the presence of Jesus, he has to ask permission. He has to go according to Jesus's plan. Jesus's will and purpose override the will of the demon. The Bible says the demons came out of the man and went into a large herd of pigs. The pigs went crazy and jumped off a cliff into the sea.

ALIVE IN CHRIST

I don't want you to let this chapter stir up a spirit of fear in you. You don't have to go around worrying about whether or not you can cancel the devil's assignments.

You don't have to pace the floor or wring your hands over the devil and his schemes. We are more than conquerors in Christ Jesus!

In Mark 5:15 the people of Gadarene heard that the demon-possessed man was healed and they came to see for themselves. The Bible says, "They came to Jesus and saw him who had been possessed with the legion of demons sitting and clothed and in his right mind. And they were afraid" (MEV). The first thing to take note of here is that the man is sitting. He had once been uncontrollable, but he regained control of himself and was sitting in the presence of Jesus.

When we get into the presence of Jesus, He will give us control over those things in our lives that have been uncontrollable. When you step away from the devil and draw close to Jesus, He will put you in your right mind. Sin will lose its attraction. You will die to sin and become alive in Christ. But this death to sin isn't always easy. Just like the people of Gadarene who got upset with Jesus when their pigs ran off the cliff, we too get upset at the thought of giving up our sinful behaviors. Sometimes we are so far from the presence of God that we would rather cling to our sin than come close to Jesus. Before their sin killed the people of Gadarene, Jesus killed their sin, but they couldn't see it that way. You can't have Jesus as Lord and keep your sins. You can't be alive in Christ if you're dying in the grip of sin.

Jesus is calling us to come into His presence, to come close. He doesn't want us sitting on the bank of the Jordan somewhere, hanging out on the border, in a state of compromise. He is inviting each one of us to come into the holy of holies and encounter His presence, to receive the life He died to give us. If you are struggling in the grip of sin, hear God calling to you. No matter how far you are from Him, it is always on His itinerary to come to you and set you free. What He did for the Gadarenes, He can do for you. Jesus can cancel the devil's assignment over your life, no matter how strong Satan's grip may be. Draw close to His presence, and He will cast all the unclean things out of your life and cancel the devil's assignment over you.

I believe our nation is a reflection of a compromised lifestyle that has left us far from the presence of God, and because of this we have set in motion intense demonic activity. If our nation will come back into the presence of God and let Him "kill our pigs"—kill our idols, our lust, our rebellion, and all of the sin that is separating us from Him—then I believe God will cancel the devil's assignment.

Learn to speak the power of God's Word and watch the devil's assignment break off your life, your family, your church, your finances, off every area of your life.

Wherever you go—before you get in your car, go into your office, board a plane—cancel the devil's assignment over you in the power of the name of Jesus. Our "weapons...are not carnal, but mighty through God to the pulling down of strongholds" (2 Cor. 10:4, KJV). What you bind or cancel on earth will be canceled in heaven (Matt 18:18). Allow God's will to be done on earth as it is in heaven in your life and come alive in Christ!

Chapter Six

MAINTAIN KINGDOM FOCUS

FTER HIS BAPTISM, Jesus spent forty days and nights in the wilderness being tempted by the devil. Satan wanted to distract Jesus from His divine purpose, and he wants to do the same with each one of us. He will use any method he can to deceive, divert, and distract. The devil will parade the most impressive material things in front of us to dazzle and distract us from the ultimate mission God has for our lives.

Far too often we make Satan's job easy for him because we are easily distracted. We seem to lose our kingdom focus without even noticing. When we continue comfortably for months without a fresh sense of the Holy Spirit in our lives, we've been distracted by the devil. When it no longer hurts to have empty altars in our churches, when we spend our time and energy debating how best to perpetuate the church rather than how to best reach the world for Jesus Christ, when the leaders of our churches become prayerless and are no longer rooted in the Word of God, we have been distracted by the devil. Without our realizing it, a spiritual church becomes a social club, a carnal church.

EMOTIONAL DISTRACTION

I have personally experienced three ways that the devil has tried to distract me from the important purposes of God. The first type of distraction I've watched the enemy use through the years is emotional distraction. When we get all worked up, but it really doesn't have anything to do with that which is eternal, that's an emotional distraction. Let me share an example of when this happened to me.

Years ago, I remember very clearly, a certain politician who was doing things that I believed were diametrically opposed to the Word of God. One week in particular I got very upset by his behavior. I got busy gathering newspaper clippings and then went to my office and shut myself in to write Sunday's sermon. I was going to tell the congregation how America was going to hell in a hand basket. But before I preached that sermon, the Lord checked my heart and showed me a truth in His Word.

He reminded me of 1 Corinthians 2:2–5, where Paul declares that he will only preach Christ and Him crucified. At this time in history the Romans were persecuting Christians in the most hideous ways. The Roman emperor Nero would tar Christians, then attach them to poles and burn them alive as lanterns along the streets of Rome, yet not once do we read of Paul blasting the Roman leadership or trying to rally a new political party. Paul understood that his primary purpose was to deliver people to the foot of the cross, and that is our primary purpose as well. The devil will try and distract us from that purpose whenever and wherever he can, and there's plenty to be distracted by in today's world. There are gross social injustices, abortion, gay marriage, racism, and the list goes on. We must stand firm on what the Scripture says about these things but refuse to be drawn into battles on these issues. Because if we're not careful, Satan will use these things to distract the church from its true mission of leading people to Christ.

The church is not called to be a political force in the earth. We are not called just to be good people who do good things. The real mission of the church is to preach Christ and Him crucified. We are not to preach denominations, political parties, or opinions. We are to preach Jesus! We must tell the world that Jesus is the Son of God and that He was born to a virgin by the name of Mary. We must share that He lived a sinless life and that He died on a bloody cross. We must explain that they buried Him in a tomb, but on the third day He rose again, and soon He's coming back.

And we must never allow the enemy to lure us away from this!

Satan will use emotional distractions to alienate us from reaching the very people that need to hear the good news of the gospel of Jesus Christ. If we're not careful, we just build a society inside of a society called "the church," and we end up reaching no one and accomplishing nothing. I often hear people say things such as, "I want to quit my job and go into the ministry so I can win souls." Let me help you understand something: all the unsaved people are out there where you work and live. Don't abandon your post. Be a minister right where you are. Win someone for Jesus without being distracted from the purpose of God.

I have seen how the enemy has tried to distract me with new methods and new philosophies over the years, trying to get my focus off the kingdom. I've had to remind myself that I'm not called to be a counselor; I'm not called to be a doctor who gives you some kind of philosophy that helps you get along in life. I am called to deal with eternal souls who face eternal consequences. It is a heavy burden. It is not a nine-to-five job. I can't leave it "at the office," and I can't afford to be distracted. There is too much at stake. The same is true for you. The enemy will do everything he can to distract you from the Word of God and from prayer. Anything in your life that is pulling you away from intimacy with Jesus is a distraction from the enemy. Hold fast to knowing nothing but Christ and Him crucified and you will be able to maintain your kingdom focus.

Opportunity Distraction

The second kind of distraction I've seen the devil try to use in my life is what I call "opportunity distraction." We all need jobs, and I believe God wants to increase us and enlarge our territories. When new opportunities present themselves, you should explore them, always keeping in mind that as believers you are to focus your heart on the call and the purpose of God for your life, not on the things of this world. Just be aware that not every seemingly good opportunity is from God. Exercise discernment when considering a major change in life, otherwise you could fall victim to one of Satan's opportunity distractions. Let me give you an example of an opportunity distraction that I've seen often over the years.

When the Spirit of God moves upon people—let's say it's a young married couple, and an amazingly anointed service touches them. They get up, walk down to the altar, clap their hands, weep profusely, and cry out to God. They've been touched and anointed by the Holy Spirit. The next thing you know, they're involved in everything going on at church—every service, every all-night prayer meeting, every home cell group—they can't get enough! They're on fire, and they start working like you've never seen anybody work. All of this is well and good until the opportunity distraction comes along. That's when I'll find them in my office saying, "Pastor, we need you to pray. Our heart is torn. This church is our life, but the Lord has given us a promotion. We can make three times what we're making. Of course it's going to require us to relocate, we've got to go away, but praise the Lord! Increase is mine!"

Suddenly it's about the money. "Have you been there on a weekend and found a church?" I ask them. "If God's really in it, there will be a provision spiritually for you," I say.

Oh, how I wish people would think a little more about God before they leap at the money. Let me say something very important right now—never move for money! Let me say it again—never, never, never, never move for money. Move because God wants you to move. Seek *first* the kingdom, and all these things will follow you. Understand that not all opportunities are of God. Too many times the devil dangles a golden carrot out in front of us; he paints some beautiful portrait of prosperity somewhere else, and we forget about what God's doing right where we are. Sometimes God will give us what you want, but He'll send a leanness of soul. You'll have money in your pocket, but you'll be empty in your soul.

It's far more important to keep your family together, to keep your children on fire for the Lord, to keep your own spirit ready for the coming of the Lord Jesus Christ, than to follow the money. These things are more valuable than a big job and more money, more important than climbing the corporate ladder.

Opportunity distractions don't always involve a move. I have people who come to me and say, "Well, Pastor, I have this great opportunity, and we don't have to move. My pay will increase tremendously, and we'll get all the stuff we want. Now, of course, I'll have to give up church because my hours will be on Sundays and Wednesdays. What should I do?" The answer is simple: if it means *less* God and *more* money, don't do it! Always go for *more* of God, and you will get everything else you need, because He's *Jehovah Jireh* (the God who provides). David knew what he was talking about when he said, "I would rather be a doorkeeper in the house of my God than dwell in the tents of wickedness" (Ps. 84:10, NKJV).

When Jesus was in the wilderness, fasting for forty days, Satan offered distractions to try and draw Him away from God's purpose. The devil came to Him and told Him there was an easier way. He didn't have to spend all that time praying, put Himself through all that. "I'll give you everything you want," he said, "if you'll just bow down and worship me. I'm sure some of you reading this have been tempted with that same opportunity distraction—just take the easy way and you can have everything you want and more.

What was Jesus's response? He said, "It is written, man shall not live by bread alone, but by every word that proceeds out of the mouth of God." In other words, bread and material things are not to be the sole purpose of life. The sole purpose of life is the fresh manna from the ovens of heaven that are in my soul. Because when I'm getting *fresh manna from heaven,* I have something even more important than bread on my table. I have the bread of life.

I have lost count of the times people have come to me and said, "Here's a business deal, and you should definitely get involved in it. Sign here, here, here, and here." If I had jumped at those opportunity distractions, I would have lost my ministry and my anointing. At some point each one of us have to choose. The Bible says, "No man that warreth entangleth himself with the affairs of this life; that he may please him who hath chosen him to be a soldier" (2 Tim. 2:4, KJV). We must keep our focus on the things of the kingdom, for that is where our true treasure is to be found.

People Distraction

In my mind "people distraction" can be the biggest distraction Satan throws at us to get us out of our victory. He will send people into our lives who will try and distract us from what God is calling us to do. It all starts with whom you trust. The Bible gives great examples of what we are to look for in those we trust. In 3 John we find three men: Gaius, who was generous in hospitality; Demetrius, who was full of good works and of a good reputation; and Diotrephes, who loved "preeminence among them [the brethren]" (v. 9, NKJV). I believe Diotrephes was one of those we find in the church who have a hefty tithe check and use it to try to influence and manipulate the leadership of the church. They may be well meaning but they just don't understand how things work in the kingdom of God.

Choosing to trust the wrong person can be one of the biggest mistakes you'll make in life, especially if you are a pastor. Hear me young pastors and young ministry leaders when I say, seek the discernment of the Holy Spirit and don't be distracted by people who tell you they were with you and were sent by God to help you. Their big cars and their big words of praise can distract you. "You're the best thing since cherry pie," they cry. "You're the most anointed person I've ever seen in my life. Let me tell you how God has sent me to help you!"

Beware! When people shower you with praise and want to be your new best friend, proceed with caution. They may be a distraction of the enemy. You may find out the hard way that they don't have the spirit of a servant; they just want the preeminence. They want to be noticed. Keep your eyes fixed on Jesus and your ears tuned to the Holy Spirit and you will always find yourself walking down the right path with the right people.

I have people come to me and say, "Well, Pastor, I'm going to marry him." "Did you consult with the Lord about this?" I ask. "Because if not, you might wake up one day and realize you've married someone who doesn't care anything at all about the cost of following Jesus." You see, the devil will bring people into your life who look like the right people, sound like the right people, and act like the right people, but they are the *wrong* people, and they can derail your life.

Aside from the wrong people who can derail you, there are any number of ways that even the right people in your life can cause distractions that can steal your attention: interruptions, crises, disagreements, phone calls, e-mails, text messages, Twitter, Facebook—in fact, social media is one giant people distraction! Watch out. When I get bombarded with people distractions,

I've found it's often right when we're about to break into a mighty revival. Or it will happen right after a great move of the Spirit. Sometimes I can almost sit and count the seconds until it happens: a powerful move of God on Sunday, and…wait for it…wait for it…somebody's mad by Monday.

The Gibeonites in the Book of Joshua are an excellent example of "people distractions." In Joshua 9 we find Joshua who has defeated Ai. When the other leaders in the area hear how powerful he is, they bring "bags of vittles." In other words, they brought little bags of goods, or little sacks of money. "We want to be your servants," they said. "We want to be your friends." The elders of Israel fell for it. They made a league with the Gibeonites without consulting the Lord, and things did not go well. When the Israelites made a league with these Gibeonites and let them travel and become a part of them, the Gibeonites continually had to be managed and defended. If Gibeon ever got in a fight with somebody, Israel had to come fight for them. Israel had to spend time and resources managing and defending these "friends" for the rest of their existence. And that's what happens to us. We let the wrong people in. We take the job that keeps us away from the house of God. We jump on the latest political bandwagon. Then we have to spend our time and resources to manage it, and we have to defend why it's there all the time. We don't have time to be about our Father's business. We don't have time to focus on the things that matter for eternity.

A GLORIOUS BRIDE

If you're tired of people distractions, opportunity distractions, and emotional distractions, you have to make up your mind, like Paul, that you're going to cast the devil out and stay on track with God. There are always distracting spirits that will come to pull you off course from what God has called you to do; people, opportunities, and even emotional ties to things will get you off course. If this is happening to you, it's time to put on your combat boots and kick the devil out of your life! Lift up your hands and say, "Lord, I surrender to Your will."

I'm not talking about whether you go to church all the time; I'm talking about your heart condition. Proverbs 4:23 says, "Guard your heart" (NIV). The deceitfulness of riches and the cares of this life choke out fruitfulness (Matt. 13:22). The disposition of your heart means more to God than big buildings, fancy churches, and plush campuses. He is looking for hearts that will break before Him and make vows of commitment not to be distracted from eternity. That's what pleases the Lord; that's the church Jesus is coming back for. I have news for you; He isn't coming back for some old bride that's had her teeth knocked out by the devil, wearing an old, dirty dress. Jesus is coming back for a glorious bride who is radiant with love for Him. When she walks in the door, the whole world is going to look in amazement at her glory and her purity. When she walks down the aisle and turns around, she's going to pull her dress up just a little, and she's going to be wearing combat boots!

Chapter Seven

LIVING LIFE WITHOUT LIMITS

T HE SPIRIT OF limitation says, "I know that the blessings of God are real. I know that the Holy Spirit's power is real, that miracles are real, that healing is real, that prosperity is real. I know that it exists, but it's not for me." That's the devil putting limitation on your life. If you let him, Satan will put a ceiling over you that says, "You can go this far but no farther. You can have this much but no more. You can succeed to this degree, but you peaked, and you're not going any higher." That's the limiting spirit of the enemy. If you're not careful, and begin to believe the lies of the enemy, you'll begin to accept his limitations. Then, when the Holy Spirit says, "Come a little farther…do a little more…expand just a little bit," you won't have the faith to follow Him.

When Jesus came into your heart, you might have been anchored to an addiction or chained to alcohol or failure, but thanks to Him, you are not that person anymore. Satan will try and limit you by reminding you of your past, whispering things such as, "Nobody in your family ever had a successful marriage. You can't expect to have a good marriage that lasts for life. Don't you even think it..." But you are not limited by your past. Throw off those chains! Don't accept the devil's limits! Don't believe his lies!

The enemy wants you to stay defeated, to put your head down. He wants you to hide in a foxhole because everything's rough. But the Lord has a remedy for those who have been limited: He wants to enlarge the place of your dwelling, and He wants you to believe Him for greater things. If you find yourself unable to worship, or holding back your tithes and offerings and limiting your giving, know that the enemy is trying to take hold of you. Break his limitations by giving more than you've ever given before. Worship with abandon. Honor the Lord with all that you have and all that you are.

Don't fall into the trap of speaking limitations over your life. Psalm 78 says they "limited the Holy One of Israel" (v. 41) when they said, "Can God prepare a table in the wilderness [in this economy]?" (v. 19, NKJV). Believe that God "can" instead of asking, "Can God?" Let your words multiply God's blessings in your life instead of setting limits. Pay attention to what you speak. Do you speak lack? Do you speak limitation? Do you speak recession? Do you speak bankruptcy? Do you speak disease? Do you speak fear? Do you speak defeat? Then guess what: you're multiplying that thing that you have spoken in your life. Your words are multipliers. The Bible says, "Death and life are in the power of the tongue" (Prov. 18:21, MEV). Instead of asking, "Can God?" say, "God can!" Start declaring God's blessings over your life: "God can spread a table for me, God can bless me in the midst of a downturn, God can free me from every limitation," and then live your life believing in God.

STOP CHASING DONKEYS AND START CHASING GOD

The enemy wants to limit your life by weighing you down with baggage. In 1 Samuel we find Saul, a tall, handsome young man from the tribe of Benjamin. One day his father, Kish, asked him to go with a servant to find some donkeys that had broken loose from their pen. Saul and the servant searched all day and night and could not find those donkeys. Saul wanted to give up, but the servant told him about a prophet in the city who might be able to help, and so they went and found the prophet.

While Saul and his servant were making their way toward the gates of the city, the Spirit of the Lord came upon the Prophet Samuel, whom they were headed to see. The Lord told him to rise up and go to the gate, where he would meet the man he would anoint as the first king of Israel. So Samuel went to the gate and began to watch the people. The moment he laid eyes upon Saul, the Holy Spirit confirmed in his heart that Saul was the man, so Samuel introduced himself and invited Saul to eat with him and stay the night.

The next morning they got up and went to the gate of the city to wait. Now, keep in mind; Saul's life was about to change forever, but he was still focused on those lost donkeys. Samuel told him, "Do not be anxious about them, for they have been found" (1 Sam. 9:20, NKJV). God had something much bigger for Saul than chasing donkeys. We can miss what God has for us because we're chasing trivial things. The enemy wants us to stay anxious, to keep us occupied with trivial things—donkey chasing—instead of God chasing.

I believe the Lord has a word for every one of you reading this book. I believe He wants you to know that He has already taken care of the issues of your life. You may have no idea how God is about to use you, but you can be sure that the enemy wants to limit you. God has amazing things planned for you. Don't make the mistake of getting caught up chasing donkeys because *you* are headed for the throne. You are a king in the kingdom of God. The Lord wants you to know that there are many people who miss great opportunities because they are distracted chasing other things. Those other things might be a person, a mistake, a temptation, or a job. There are always donkeys to chase that will pull you away from what God has for you. If you allow them, they will rob you of your kingship. Don't let your baggage keep you from God's best.

Samuel anointed Saul at the gate and declared he would be king, and true to God's word, a few months later the big day came when all of Israel gathered by the tens of thousands to crown Saul as the first king of Israel. It was a huge celebration. The men were celebrating in the streets; the women were dancing with timbrels and tambourines; the children had streamers in their hands. There was one problem—Saul was nowhere to be found. So they announced his name again, but still he did not come forth.

"Therefore they inquired of the LORD further, 'Has the man come here yet?' And the LORD answered, 'There he is, hidden among the equipment'" (1 Sam. 10:22, NKJV). The word *equipment* was originally the term for *baggage*. Saul's big day arrived, and he was so weighed down with baggage that he could not step in to what God was calling him to do. Instead he went and hid. Any one of us can miss what God has for us if we aren't willing to let go of our baggage. This is one of the ways the enemy puts limitations on your life, to keep you from receiving the blessings of God. You have to stop chasing donkeys that don't really matter in the big picture of God's plan for your life, because that kind of baggage from the past will hold you back from your calling. It is not about your strength or your ability; it's about trusting God.

Baggage can come from false teaching, lack of understanding, even from inside your own family. We must learn to step out of that stuff, leave the baggage behind, stop being a donkey chaser and become a God chaser. Run after the promises of God. Step out of the limits of the enemy and into God's unlimited favor. The choice is yours—choose to live in freedom, in God's embrace.

Throw Away the Duct Tape

Some of you may recognize the term "duct-tape faith" from a message I preached about the four horns of Zechariah 1:17–21. I also mention it in my book *Believe That You Can*. But for those who have never heard of duct-tape faith, let me explain. I got the idea of duct-tape faith at a time when our television ministry was struggling. One day as I waited in our studio for the crew to set up so I could record for an upcoming program, I looked around and noticed that there was duct tape on everything. Duct tape held the lenses on the cameras, held the wires together. Duct tape was holding the lights in place. Even the recorders we were using to make copies were all duct taped together. Then I noticed our television director carrying around a big wad of duct tape everywhere he went.

As I looked around, the Lord spoke to me and said, "That's the kind of faith you've got: duct-tape faith." He said, "You know why you're at duct-tape level? Because you don't believe Me for anything better than this." I remember it like it was yesterday. Right then and there I determined to break loose from the duct-tape level of living. The devil wanted me to accept things as they were, but instead I made a declaration of what God has said to me. When the cameras rolled that day I said, "Now listen. We're trying to build a sanctuary. We don't have enough money to build it, and we certainly don't have enough to buy new equipment. That's why I've got duct tape all over everything. But in Jesus's name, I believe God has told me He is going to take the duct tape off of our ministry." Within thirty days more than a million dollars came in, and we bought the latest television equipment that money can buy, and never looked back.

Some of you are living at the duct-tape level. You buy stuff on sale and then return it to another store where it's not on sale and make a little bit of money. Or you owe two bills and you don't have money for either ones, so you accidentally put the check to pay

for the gas bill in the envelope for the power company, to buy more time. I know some of you reading
this know what I'm talking about! You're living at
duct-tape level when it doesn't even cross your mind
to believe God for something better. Instead, you just
keep telling yourself, "Just hold things together a little
bit longer; just stretch these resources a little bit farther. We can't afford to fix it or replace it, so hurry and
patch it up before it falls apart. Go get the duct tape!"

The devil wants you to live at duct-tape level. He
will try and put limits on your life with a spirit of lack.
A spirit of lack presses you down and tells you that
you'll have to operate at this level the rest of your life,
because as long as you stay at duct-tape level, you aren't
a threat to the enemy. But just as soon as you lift up
your head and determine to go to the next level with
God, that old deceiving spirit of lack will show up and
try and hold you back. I've seen people let the spirit of
lack hold them in the same territory generation after
generation. Don't let that be you. Be on the lookout for
the spirit of lack. I like to joke that when you first start
out in married life, everything is wonderful; it's *ideal*.
Then, a few months later there's an *ordeal*, and before
long you're thinking, "This is a *raw deal*." That's when
the devil has you looking for a *new deal* because a
spirit of lack has come into your marriage.

Satan wants you to develop a mentality of lack,

where you never expect things to get better. Where you think God will bless others but not you. If you let him, he'll hit you with a lack attack in every area of your life. It's time to stop listening to the spirit of lack from the father of lies and start living with faith in the God who saved you, the One who loves you. "'For I know the plans I have for you,' declares the LORD, 'plans to prosper you and not to harm you, plans to give you hope and a future'" (Jer. 29:11, NIV).

If you are walking around with a roll of duct tape, trying to hold things together in your life, robbing Peter to pay Paul because you think God's not going to bless you, I want to encourage you to stay focused on the promises of God. It may seem easier to put duct tape on life's problems, but giving in to the lies of the devil won't make life easier. It will ruin your life. Put down that duct tape and pick up the promises of God. When the devil starts whispering his lies in your ear, tell him, "In the name of Jesus, spirit of lack, it's not legal for you to be in my life. I serve a God of abundance. I serve a God of more than enough. I know what His Word has promised to me. I will praise Him in spite of my circumstances."

When life gets difficult, refuse to listen to the lies of the devil that try and tell you that your business is going under, or your kids are never going to serve God, or you'll never regain your health. I want you to know that you can expect God to come through for you. You can break the devil's grip on your life in the mighty name of Jesus, conquering the very thing that was out to conquer you, for we are more than conquerors in Christ Jesus (Rom. 8:31–39). God has made provision for your victory and success in life. "But thank God! He gives us victory over sin and death through our Lord Jesus Christ" (1 Cor. 15:57, NLT). *Refuse to let the enemy prohibit your growth. Refuse to allow your present circumstances to limit your faith or dictate your future. Allow God to dictate your future instead. Start living a life without limits through the One who lives within you, Jesus Christ.*

Often, when we are going through difficulties in life, we become so discouraged we begin to lose faith and start asking questions such as, "If God is with me, why does He let these things happen to me?" This might surprise you, but God being with you has nothing to do with having a perfect life. Life in general is a battle, however, when God is with you, you are no longer fighting the battle in your own limited strength, but in His unlimited strength. Know that God wants to take you to a new level, one beyond duct-tape faith. You just have to trust Him to carry you through. Press in to His presence and trust Him, even in difficult times, and He *will* come through for you.

LIVE ACCORDING TO GOD'S DEFINITION OF "BIG"

Did you know that there's this concept in your mind that defines "big" in your life? If I say something like, "Big money, big church, or big success," you have a good idea of what those things look like. The problem is, we are often unknowingly in the habit of letting Satan define "big" instead of living according to God's definition of "big."

Let me explain. In every level of ministry that I've experienced, at some point I've had to get past what I thought was big. When I was growing up, my dad never pastored big, big churches, so in my mind, when the church I was pastoring hit seven hundred people, I thought, "Whoa, this is big!" Looking back on it now, I can see that the church stayed at that level for a while because I accepted the limitations the enemy put on my faith.

Recently I found an old newsletter I had written in 1993. In it I said, "We really need to pray. We're starting our first twenty-one-day fast. Here's what we're fasting for. We've got three hundred fifty empty seats in the new sanctuary." I didn't realize it at the time, but I was struggling to have enough faith for what I considered to be big. There were three sections in the balcony that were empty, and my idea of big was so limited that I had difficulty imaging them filled with people. My thinking was limited.

But thankfully God didn't leave me in that place of limited thinking. He began to build up my faith, through His Word, through prophecies, and in times of prayer. Then we moved into a new building, and I thought it was big until we filled it up. Then we added our California campus, and it too filled up. Now we have a third campus and that is filling up too. Every time I thought, "This is big," God caused my faith to go up another notch. Through it all I had to push against the devil's grip on my faith, and my dreams, and my vision. It was when my faith saw it done, it happened.

You have to push against the limitations of the enemy. I talk about building and expanding the ministry all the time, because I refuse to let the devil limit my thinking. Some people look at me as if I'm crazy, but I refuse to deal with the spirit of limitation. By exercising my faith to get past what *I* think is big, I break into God's definition of big, because I want to live in God's definition of life, not the devil's.

I challenge you today to look with eyes of faith beyond the limits of what you think is big for your life and begin to declare God's definition of life without limits over your marriage, your family, your business, your career, your finances, your health, your ministry. Speak words of increase with faith that God will bring the increase in your life. God says, "When your faith is ready, I'm ready." Start today, pushing against those limitations. Put down the duct tape. It's time for a new harvest to come in your life. Break off what has been limiting you, push past what you think is big. God is waiting to enlarge your territory. He wants to increase you and prosper you so you can increase His kingdom.

MATURE IN CHRIST

There are two spiritual seasons in our lives that I call "whens." In his letter to the Corinthians, Paul writes, "*When* I was a child, I spoke as a child, I understood as a child, I thought as a child. But *when* I became a man, I put away childish things" (1 Cor. 13:11, MEV, emphasis added).

When you are born again into God's family you experience the first "when." This is your spiritual childhood stage so to speak, during which you grow in your relationship with God by reading and studying His Word and talking to Him in prayer. In this stage you learn how to walk and live by faith from teachers of His Word. As you learn God's ways you become more familiar with what love, peace, and purity mean in the kingdom of God.

At some point you should find yourself in your second "when," which is spiritual adulthood. You are now a mature Christian, someone who gives witness to Jesus's love and what He's done for you as you lead others to Christ. Unfortunately many of us never get past our spiritual childhood because we get stuck in the past. We cling to our old, carnal ways rather than leaving them behind and walking in God's ways.

It is not God's desire or design that we remain stuck in the past, ensnared by our carnal desires and behaviors. God intends for us to become fully mature in Christ so we can produce His kingdom fruit. We can grow and change from glory to glory in our relationship with Jesus, in our love walk, and in our worship and prayer time. But how do we do that?

As I reflected on Paul's words in 1 Corinthians 13:11, the Lord gave me a simple thought. Catching your second "when" requires sanctification. We can't move from the "when" of spiritual childhood to the "when" of spiritual adulthood in our own strength. The transition comes when we yield to God and allow Him to set us apart (sanctify) us.

Perhaps you're born again. You're in God's kingdom, but you're stuck. You just can't seem to get your second "when." You have somehow settled for the mediocrity of the first "when." But there is so much more God wants to do in you and through you, and therein we find the crux of the matter—God has marvelous plans for you, and Satan wants to thwart those plans. He wants to keep us stuck in our past. He wants to keep us caught up in guilt and shame, replaying the mistakes and failures of our past instead of leaving them at the cross and moving on with God. Understand that Satan is not creative. If the devil keeps reminding you of your past, it's because he's running out of new material!

God never runs out of new material. He offers us new life, which includes closing the book on the past. Jesus died so that we can be free of the sin that tries to ensnare us, both the old sin and the new. Make no mistake, one of Satan's greatest ploys is to blind us to the cross. I want to say something loud and clear: "He has now reconciled you in His fleshly body through death, in order to present you before Him holy and blameless and beyond reproach" (Col. 1:22, NAS). In Isaiah 43:25 God says "I, even I, am he who blots out your transgressions, for my own sake, and remembers your sins no more" (NIV). If God is not remembering your sins, why should you?

There's a passage in Colossians 2:14 that thrills me every time I read it: "Having canceled out the certificate of debt consisting of decrees against us, which was hostile to us; and He has taken it out of the way, having nailed it to the cross" (NAS). Whenever a person would be convicted in a Roman court, a certificate of debt would be prepared. It was a list of every crime the person was accused of committing. It would then be taken with the prisoner to wherever he would be imprisoned and nailed to the door of the cell. This analogy from Paul illustrates how God dealt with our sins. When Jesus hung on the cross two thousand years ago, the certificate of debt of every person who would ever live was nailed to the cross with Him. Jesus took our certificate of debt and nailed it to the cross to pay the debt of our sin.

According to Roman law when someone was thrown in prison and their certificate of debt nailed to the door, it remained there until the sentence was carried out. Then the word meaning "IT IS FINISHED" was written across the certificate, and it was rolled up and given to the prisoner. In that way no one could be punished for that particular crime again.

Before Jesus bowed His head on the cross and said, "Father, into Your hands I commit My spirit" (Luke 23:46, MEV), He gave a victory cry and said, "It is finished!" (John 19:30, MEV). The Greek word for this is *teleo*, meaning "paid in full." Jesus took our certificate of debt and wrote across it with His own blood, "It is finished," paid in full. That means that we have received God's full pardon. Our sins have been nailed to the cross, taken care of forever, so that we can live the life without limits that God intends for each one of us.

Too many have been in church for years but are still in the "childhood" stage. That is not natural. Hebrews 9:14 says, "How much more shall the blood of Christ... cleanse your conscience from dead works to serve the living God?" (NKJV). Let the blood of Jesus

Christ cleanse your conscience from the guilt of sin so that you may walk in the new authority and understand who you are in Christ.

Before the Prophet Samuel was born, his mother prayed for a child who she promised to dedicate to the Lord. God answered her prayers and gave her a son. When Samuel was just a child, he went to live in the temple so that he might learn to hear from God and so that God could minister to him. Each year his mother would return to the temple with a new suit of clothing for her son because he was growing. Samuel started out as a child and he grew, not just physically, but also spiritually. That's a picture of what God wants for your life. He doesn't intend for you to stay in the temple forever. Your time in the temple is preparation for your second "when," but there comes a time when you outgrow the garments of childhood and need to move on to the clothing of adulthood. God has bigger things for you, bigger garments so to speak. He has left your past at the cross, and you are not to go back and pick it up! Leave the old behind, pressing on toward new life in Christ; toward a limitless life!

God Is With Us

Life in the kingdom is life without limits, but the devil will always try and tell you otherwise. He will try and convince you that God isn't really with you, that you are actually quite limited. Perhaps you have come from a really dysfunctional family. You are growing spiritually, but there is always this nagging voice that is telling you that God isn't going to use you because your family was such a mess and you're going to turn out the same way. That's a lie of the enemy. God fixes dysfunction. He is the ultimate dysfunction fixer.

Think about Joseph and his family. Joseph's father's name was Jacob, which means *cheater*. He had lied and cheated, and everybody knew it. On top of that, Joseph had brothers who tried to kill him because he wore a different coat. He was thrown into a pit, lied about by Mrs. Potiphar, forgotten by his friends, passed over, and abused. But in spite of all this, Joseph had such a relationship with God that he grew spiritually anyway. His family's dysfunction didn't hold him back. When Potiphar's wife tried to seduce him, Joseph refused her advances because he had God's commands written on his heart. Notice that God continued to bless Joseph as he continued to grow spiritually.

Now God blessed Joseph with a wife and a child, and they named him Manasseh, which in Hebrew means, "The Lord has made me to forget." Instead of giving his son a name that reflected the torment of his past, Joseph named his son for the victory of his future. Joseph had learned it is not what has been done to you, and it is not what you have done, but it is what you *will do* that counts with God.

David had some dysfunction in his family too. In Psalm 51:5 David wrote, "Behold, I was brought forth in iniquity, and in sin my mother conceived me" (NKJV). From this verse some Bible commentators believe that David was an illegitimate child. They claim that was the reason David was left out when Samuel told Jesse to bring all his boys for review. Jesse only brought seven out of the eight, leaving David behind because he was not a legitimate son. Regardless of his past, David continued to seek the Lord, longing to know Him and please Him, and as a result, he became stronger as he grew and matured.

If the enemy has been tormenting you with your past, trying to convince you that God isn't really with you, don't believe him! Your past is just that—the past. God isn't focusing on your past so why should you? You have another chance with God, and this time the outcome isn't dependent on what you do in your own strength, but what God does in you and through you. David was able to slay the giant because he knew who God was, and that is where he put his focus, not on the fact that he was a skinny little kid coming up against a giant who had been terrorizing the whole arm of Israel. What giants are you facing? Allow God to order your steps and trust Him to back you with

His strength the moment you are faithful to follow through. David heard the taunts of that giant and said to King Saul:

> "Your servant used to keep his father's sheep, and when a lion or a bear came and took a lamb out of the flock, I went out after it and struck it, and delivered the lamb from its mouth; and when it arose against me, I caught it by its beard, and struck and killed it. Your servant has killed both lion and bear; and this uncircumcised Philistine will be like one of them, seeing he has defied the armies of the living God." Moreover David said, "The LORD, who delivered me from the paw of the lion and from the paw of the bear, He will deliver me from the hand of this Philistine."
> —1 SAMUEL 17:34–37, NKJV

David was fully aware that God empowered him to protect his flock and rescue the young lamb from the mouth of the predator. He knew it would be no different with that ridiculous giant. The Israelite army was measuring the giant's threats against their own strength and power. David was measuring against his omnipotent God of all creation. In our weakness He is always strong. God doesn't need your strength. He wants your weakness and dependency on Him. Goliath was bigger than David, but if the God in you is bigger than the devil in them, it does not matter how big the circumstance. You will win.

God is with you, and He wants to take you to a new level, but you must be hungry for it and put away childish things. Build your prayer life with persistence and faithfulness, read your Bible daily, develop a fasting lifestyle, and worship often. Grow in your knowledge and love of Christ and His kingdom until you are fully "grown up" in Christ.

I've often heard the words of Jesus taken out of context when He asked, "When the Son of Man comes, will He really find faith on the earth?" It helps to see that verse in context. In Luke 18:1–8 Jesus was speaking to a group of Pharisees and His disciples.

> Then He spoke a parable to them, that men always ought to pray and not lose heart, saying: "There was in a certain city a judge who did not fear God nor regard man. Now there was a widow in that city; and she came to him, saying, 'Get justice for me from my adversary.' And he would not for a while; but afterward he said within himself, 'Though I do not fear God nor regard man, yet because this widow troubles me I will avenge her, lest by her continual coming she weary me.'" Then the Lord said, "Hear what the unjust judge said. And shall God not avenge His own elect who cry out day and night to Him,

though He bears long with them? I tell you that He will avenge them speedily. Nevertheless, when the Son of Man comes, will He really find faith on the earth?"

—NKJV

Notice that He began the parable as a lesson that, "Men always ought to pray and not lose heart," and ended it with the question, "When the Son of Man comes, will He really find faith on the earth?" Jesus asks us still today: "When the Son of man comes, will He find the kind of faith that persists in the face of apparent denial and delay?" When everybody else says it's over, that God has left you, will you choose to believe that God is still with you? When the enemy tries to convince you that it is over for your kids, that they will never get their act together, do you know that's not God's voice? I believe you do. I believe that you are going to reach out and take hold of God's truths. I believe you are going to get that "God is with me" spirit about your future, about your family, about your church, about everything, even your finances. No matter what crisis you may be facing right now, you cannot be victorious with the spirit of the world, but you will find victory with God because He is with you. "And surely I am with you always, to the very end of the age" (Matt. 28:20, NIV).

Chapter Eight

YOU HAVE THE KEYS

J ESUS CHRIST OPENLY subdued Satan and his minions, and God gave Him [Jesus] all rule and authority in this age and the age to come. The kingdom of heaven knows this, and the kingdom of darkness knows it. The problem is, too many Christians do not live like they know it, so they are not operating from that position of victory.

Think about this for a moment: Jesus has the keys of hell and death, so what keys does Satan still have? None! He doesn't have any keys. He doesn't even have the keys to his own kingdom anymore.

Here is how the Prophet Isaiah described the fall of Lucifer:

> How you are fallen from heaven, O Lucifer, son of the morning! How you are cut down to the ground, you who weaken the nations!…Yet you shall be brought down to Hell, to the sides of the pit. Those who see you shall stare at you and ponder over you: "Is this the man who made the

earth to tremble and shook kingdoms, who made
the world as a wilderness and destroyed its cities,
who did not open the house of his prisoners?"
—ISAIAH 14:12, 15–17, MEV

Isaiah used words such as *fallen*, *cut down*, and *brought down*. In the last verses he describes how shocked people will be when they see Satan in his defeated state—as the small, powerless demon that he is. They will probably need to squint their eyes a little to see him and wonder how he did so much damage. Satan has been defeated, but he still wreaks havoc in the world. Where then does he get his power?

The devil gets power in our lives when we give it to him. Whenever we engage in ungodly, sinful behavior, we open a door for the devil to come in. But the good news is that once we learn to identify the openings we leave for him, we can get rid of his influence, shut the door on him, and destroy his access to our lives. We don't have to be his prey. We can defeat the devil because Jesus has stripped him of all his power. The devil only has as much power in our lives as we give him.

The writer of Hebrews said that Jesus took on flesh, became like one of us, and defeated the devil (Heb. 2:14). Scripture makes it clear that Jesus stripped the devil of all power and authority through His death, burial, and resurrection: "Having disarmed principalities and powers, He made a public spectacle of them, triumphing over them in it" (Col. 2:15, NKJV). In Revelation 1:18 the Lord proclaimed that He is the one who was dead but now lives forever and holds the keys of Hades and death. As Christians, we need to learn to live from this position of victory that Jesus has won for us.

Take Off the Old, Put On the New

In Ephesians 4:22–24 the Apostle Paul was giving some how-to instructions to the church in Ephesus when he wrote, "You were taught, with regard to your former way of life, to put off your old self, which is being corrupted by its deceitful desires; to be made new in the attitude of your minds; and to put on the new self, created to be like God in true righteousness and holiness" (NIV).

Notice how Paul is giving the church three distinct steps in this passage. The first step involves *putting off the old way of life*, which has to do with lust, impurity, falsehood, lying, anger, bitterness, stealing, unwholesome talk, rage, brawling, slander and every form of malice. Second, you are to *renew your mind and put on your new self*. And right in the middle of his list, Paul gives us the third step: *"Do not give the devil a foothold"* (v. 27, NIV, emphasis added).

Rock climbers will tell you that a foothold doesn't

have to be very big. It can be just a little bump, even a small crevice. As long as it is something that you can wedge the edge of your big toe and ball of your foot against, you can use it to push yourself up to higher ground. The devil looks for footholds in a believer's life because he knows that we have been given the victory in Christ, but when we give way to him and allow a foothold, we give away that victory.

All those things Paul associated with your old self will act as footholds for the devil to gain ground, gain access, and gain *power* in your life. They open doors and windows for Satan to enter and wrap himself around your life.

Conform to the Word, Not the World

Man is made of spirit, soul, and body. Flesh gives birth to flesh that decays, but the Holy Spirit gives birth to the spirit that is eternal—our physical bodies decay, but our spirits live on. That is why Jesus explained to Nicodemus that one must be born of water and Spirit in John 3:5–6. While I do believe that disease and illness can be an assignment of the enemy, I believe that in large part we do so much damage to our bodies through our own appetites that the devil doesn't have to make our bodies his main target. Since he cannot touch our spirits, his focus is on our *souls*.

God breathed life into Adam at the creation of the world, making him a living soul. A soul is a uniquely human feature. Unlike any other creation God made, mankind has been given the ability to make choices and decisions. As I mentioned in the previous chapter, you and I make choices every day that affect the spiritual atmosphere and empower the operation of one of two kingdoms: either the kingdom of light or the kingdom of darkness.

Satan's realm of influence is in the human soul—the center of the mind, will, and emotions. The only power the devil has in this world is the power we turn over to him through our choices and actions. We empower Satan when we rebel. When we sin and follow our fleshly desires rather than the Holy Spirit, we open doors to the kingdom of darkness.

Remember the scripture from Isaiah 14 that I shared in the last chapter? Pride was found in Lucifer *before* he was the devil. He said, "I will ascend above the heights of the clouds, I will be like the Most High" (v. 14, MEV). Lucifer was a beautifully decorated angel of music. He was in the presence of God before Creation. Ezekiel 28:15 says he was perfect from the day he was created until iniquity was found in him.

You can be a Christian and still be full of pride. It is the subtlest of all sins because it is rooted in self-will. Isaiah said that like sheep we have all gone astray, and each of us has turned to his own way (Isa. 53:6). Notice that he didn't say each has turned to the devil's way, or to the world's way, but rather to *his own* way. Self-will has to do with following your own way and adhering to your own opinions and desires. For example, many people who claim to be Christians try to conform the Word of God to fit their *lives* rather than conforming their lives to the *Word of God*.

The devil wants to squeeze the very breath of God out of us by causing us to stop reading the Word, because he knows that reading God's Word is like inhaling spiritual breath. Satan is constantly trying to maneuver us into a place of idolatry (1 Sam. 15:23). If he can get us to stop reading the Word and inhaling the spiritual breath of God, he knows doubts will begin to creep in. We will start to believe certain things in the Bible, but not everything. Then we start thinking we can be a Christian but live the way we want to instead of following God's Word. That's when the devil knows he has maneuvered us into a place of self-will and stubbornness. We are now worshipping at the altar of self instead of worshipping God.

SET THE SPIRITUAL ATMOSPHERE

God placed Adam in the Garden of Eden with dominion over it to keep it prospering and protected.

When Adam discovered that the "old serpent" had been whispering to his wife, he had the authority to kick it out—but he chose not to do so. Instead, Adam chose to rebel against the specific instruction God gave him not to eat of the tree of the knowledge of good and evil (Gen. 2:17). Sin found a way into that garden and enticed Eve through her mind, will, and emotions. Eve was deceived, but not Adam. He could have put an end to it, but he joined in instead.

Genesis 3:6 tells us that Eve "saw that the tree was good for food, that it was pleasing to the eyes, and a tree desirable to make one wise" (MEV). Satan went after the soul to sway her decision. He tempted her with something better. Notice this temptation is rooted in pride, the very thing that brought him down. Take a look at your life right now. Is there a hole in the fence, a broken window, or maybe a wide-open front door? Is there pride in your life?

You have the ability to set the spiritual atmosphere in your life and your home. Whether you are single, newly married, or a parent, if you take your relationship with God seriously, God will empower you to live a life worthy of Him. It is when you don't take your God-given authority seriously that you empower the enemy. Fathers and mothers can be spiritual leaders in the family when they lead by example, exemplifying Christ. When you make decisions that empower the enemy, he is quite happy to walk in the dominion that you forfeit. The decisions we make each day will affect the spiritual atmosphere of our homes. The wisest man in the world, Solomon, said, "Like a city whose walls are broken through is a person who lacks self-control" (Prov. 25:28, NIV). When you have no self-control, you leave yourself and your home open for anything to attack. The devil doesn't even need a foot-hold in a situation like that. Demons can come and go freely through the doors you've left open to them.

TAME YOUR TONGUE

We should never make the mistake of thinking that our words are not as serious as our actions. Proverbs 18:21 clearly states, "Death and life are in the power of the tongue" (MEV). Have you ever found yourself in situations when you felt you just couldn't take anymore? Situations like that seem to justify letting someone have it, but that means you are letting un-renewed thoughts, insecurities, and unrestrained emotions lead you instead of the Spirit of God. The next thing you know, your tongue is giving power to the wrong kingdom. The enemy watches for you to lose self-control because that is a soul decision that empowers him.

The next time you're tempted to say something unwholesome, to gossip, argue, or criticize—even if it seems justified—remember that it is better to turn the issue over to God than to empower the wrong kingdom and let the devil in. The devil wants to silence your voice, and when he can't do that, he will try and corrupt what comes out of your mouth.

Take Every Thought Captive to Christ

Before Satan can overcome you, he must get a temptation in your mind. That is why the greatest battle for your soul is *not* the war going on between angels and demons; it is the war going on between your ears. When James taught about temptation, he said each of us is tempted when we are drawn away by our own desires. "Then, when desire has conceived, it gives birth to sin; and sin, when it is full-grown, brings forth death" (James 1:15, NKJV).

Satan gains access to your mind through your eyes, your ears, and your mouth. The things you allow yourself to watch, to hear, and to speak profoundly affect the spiritual atmosphere of your life. When you feel yourself tempted, take that thought and give it to Jesus. Make it conform to His gospel, to His Word, and in this way you will push the devil right out of the picture, right out of your mind!

Live in the Light

Jesus said, "The lamp of the body is the eye. If therefore your eye is good, your whole body will be full of light. But if your eye is bad, your whole body will be full of darkness. If therefore the light that is in you is darkness, how great is that darkness!" (Matt. 6:22–23, NKJV).

God sees what you do in darkness. You cannot look at pornography in the secrecy of your home office, in the dark of night, and expect the presence of God to be near you. The atmosphere you live in either attracts the presence of God or drives Him away.

What are you watching? To what and to whom are you listening? Images and thoughts will try to get in—but you don't have to let them stay. "Let the wicked forsake his way, and the unrighteous man his thoughts; and let him return to the LORD, and He will have mercy on him, and to our God, for He will abundantly pardon" (Isa. 55:7, MEV).

Choose Who You Will Empower

God did not design us to walk around defeated and oppressed. He never intended for His church to be powerless. But the church today often seems to lack the power of the early church. Why? Because we have lost sight of our authority. It is time to take the power back, to regain our authority!

We need to recognize the One in us who is greater than the enemy. It is time to humble ourselves before Him, repent of self-will, stubbornness, and everything in our lives that offers the devil a safe harbor or foothold. It is time to pray passionately and often, worship fully, and live lives worthy of Jesus Christ. It is time to empower ourselves and the church, and stop empowering the devil. Jesus promised, "For where two or three are gathered together in My name, I am there in the midst of them" (Matt. 18:20, NKJV). He is here, among us. He lives in us in the power of the Holy Spirit. He has given us authority and told us to go forth with the good news of the gospel. We just need to choose who we will empower.

BE UNASHAMED OF THE GOSPEL

Do you know when a church is its most powerful? When people become unashamed. We should never be ashamed of the power of God and the gifts of the Spirit, because they are what the world needs. When a church preaches the gospel of Jesus Christ and souls are regularly saved—that is a powerful church! When we are unashamed, we empower the kingdom of light.

Jesus is the light of the world (John 8:12), and we should be shouting this good news from every rooftop!

If God is speaking to your heart right now about things that need to be cleaned up and cleaned out, stop right now and listen to Him. He is ready to wash you and your thoughts clean so that you can set your mind on things above. Take a moment to shut out everything around you and pray this prayer, knowing that God hears you, forgives you, and will fill you with His Spirit to empower you to defeat the devil in every area of your life:

> *God, here are the secret chambers of my life. I want You to be more than the Lord of my public life. I want you to be Lord of my private life. Clean me out. Fill me with the Holy Spirit and use me for Your glory. Amen.*

Chapter Nine

IT'S ALL ABOUT RELATIONSHIP

WE ARE NOT here by chance. God breathed the breath of life into us, and created us as rational beings with the ability to choose to love and follow Him, or reject Him. In the beginning He put His mouth on a lump of clay and shared His breath with Adam, the first man, made in God's image (Gen. 2:7). The Hebrew word for "breath" in this verse is *neshamah,* which literally means "air inhaled and exhaled." God inhaled and exhaled in the garden and created man. This is the first time the Bible mentions the breath of God.

The second time the Bible mentions the breath of God is found in 2 Timothy 3:16–17, when Paul explained that "all Scripture is given by inspiration of God, and is profitable for doctrine, for reproof, for correction, for instruction in righteousness, that the man of God may be complete, thoroughly equipped for every good work" (NKJV). The word *inspiration* is translated from the Greek word *theópneustos,* (*theós*, which means "God," and *pnéo*, which means "breathe out").

The Bible is literally God-breathed. That is why it is not like any other book. The words of Scripture were divinely inspired, or "breathed out" by God through the Holy Spirit. The Apostle Peter put it this way: "No prophecy of Scripture is of any private interpretation, for prophecy never came by the will of man, but holy men of God spoke as they were moved by the Holy Spirit" (2 Pet. 1:20–21, NKJV).

Approximately forty different men put together the Bible. Isn't it amazing that the words of all the different prophets and writers of the Bible fit perfectly together over a fifteen-hundred-year span? When you think about it, most of them had no way of knowing what the others were writing, and yet all of them say the same thing, because God breathed life into His Book, making the shadows and types fit perfectly together. Men like Moses, and the prophets, and the disciples all experienced the breath of God; His divine anointing allowed His heart to be recorded for all eternity.

And then He sent His Son, Jesus, who opened the way for the Holy Spirit to be *in* the people of God. Just as God breathed life into Adam in the beginning, Jesus breathed on His disciples. After His resurrection, Jesus appeared first to Mary Magdalene in the garden, and then to the disciples in an upper room. There, He spoke to them, commissioning them to be His witnesses, as His spoken words went forth with anointing and power. "He breathed on them and said, 'Receive the Holy Spirit'" (John 20:22, NIV).

We can't keep God's Word in the natural. It is the power of the Holy Spirit that enables us to live supernaturally, so that we can both *hear* the Word and *do* the Word. It takes the breath of God in us, filling us with His life, in order to keep His commandments. It is not possible for us to change so that we are deserving of God's grace and goodness. We must be born again and receive His breath of life through the Holy Spirit for true change to take place.

When Ezekiel was given the vision of the valley of dry bones, he looked upon that which was lifeless, and in his flesh there was nothing he could do. But God said to him, "Prophesy to these bones and say to them, 'Dry bones, hear the word of the LORD! This is what the Sovereign LORD says to these bones: I will make breath enter you, and you will come to life.... Then you will know that I am the LORD'" (Ezekiel 37:4–6, NIV). While there are several interpretations of this passage pertaining to Israel and the church in the end times, I also see another meaning. I see God demonstrating how He can breathe life into dead, hopeless situations. Through Him, with His breath in us, we are overcomers. The voice of the enemy may try and whisper lies of despair and hopelessness in our ear, but the life-giving breath of God is *in* us to bring victory. It is in God's power that we can live life abundantly.

RELATIONSHIP BRINGS LIFE

God created us to be in relationship with Him, yet sadly many believers don't understand what this means. They might experience God for a few moments during a worship service, but in all the other hours and minutes of their day they don't know how to connect with God in true intimacy. Without physical breath, our bodies die. It is the same with our spirit; without spiritual breath, our spirit man dies. Reading the Bible is like breathing God's breath into our spirit. We must learn how to inhale God's spiritual breath through His Word, and exhale His breath in our prayers.

Jesus modeled the kind of relationship we are to have with God. The Gospels tell us of the many times He would draw away from the crowds in order to spend time with His heavenly Father. He knew that to stay connected to the Father is to stay connected to the source of all life. Jesus did nothing without first talking with God. "Most assuredly, I say to you, the Son can do nothing of Himself, but what He sees the Father do; for whatever He does, the Son also does in like manner. For the Father loves the Son, and shows Him all things that He Himself does; and He will show

Him greater works than these, that you may marvel" (John 5:19–20, NKJV).

Many have a concept of Jesus being so much of God that He never struggled with the same kind of problems we face, but that is not what the Bible tells us. Jesus was fully God and fully man (Heb. 2:5–18), able to sympathize with our weaknesses because He was tempted in the same ways, although He did not fall into sin (Heb. 4:15). He understands that life can be an emotional roller coaster. He knows that Satan is constantly tempting us to live according to our flesh rather than according to God's Spirit. And Jesus knows that in order to resist the devil and his schemes, we have to maintain a close relationship with the Father. Jesus's life is living proof that we can develop the same intimacy with the Father that He had, if we choose. He is our pattern and our example.

God desires an intimate relationship with us. He wants us so close, we can "feel" His breath, breathe Him in. Satan knows this; he knows the power of an intimate relationship with God and will do everything he can to keep us from such a relationship. Be careful who you share the intimate things of your spirit with. We must stay in the Word, pray constantly, and press in to God in every way, every day, so that we can live the limitless life God intends for every believer.

Three Characteristics of Godly Relationships

Intimacy, dependency, and obedience are the three distinct characteristics that marked Jesus's earthly relationship with God. These three characteristics can be found in the lives of others in the Bible as well—Moses, David, John, and Paul for instance. So what would it look like to have those qualities in your life as well? Let's begin with intimacy.

Intimacy

During Jesus's earthly ministry multitudes followed Him because of the miracles He performed. Then one day He invited them to be even closer. "I am the bread of life." He told them. "Your ancestors ate the manna in the wilderness, yet they died. But here is the bread that comes down from heaven, which anyone may eat and not die. I am the living bread that came down from heaven. Whoever eats of this bread will live forever. This bread is my flesh, which I will give for the life of the world" (John 6:48–51, NIV).

These words from Jesus were more than many could handle, and Scripture tells us that at that point many of His disciples turned away and no longer followed Him. Twelve disciples remained, and He chose to pour His life and teaching into them. Out of those twelve there were three who became even closer. And out of the three there was one, "John the beloved," who laid his head on Jesus's chest at their last meal together—close enough to hear the Lord's heart beating.

Intimacy with the Lord requires alone time with just Him. I have a level of relationship with God in public, behind the pulpit, and with my family and friends, but intimacy with God requires time alone with just Him, time to seek His presence, one-on-one. It is out of intimacy that relationship flows. If you want to know God's will for your life, spend time with Him. Draw near to God, and He will draw near to you (James 4:8).

The Three Ds of Intimacy

God has given us three keys to intimacy with Him; three things that will help us develop a close relationship with Him. They are desire, discipline, and delight.

- Desire

   We must desire intimacy with God above all else. When the Father sees this desire in our hearts, He will begin to reveal Himself as we fellowship with Him. As I said earlier, establish a place of meeting and wait for God there. It is in this secret place that He will reveal His will and plans for your life. Don't expect God to shout out His plans for you; go to that quiet place and listen, and you will hear Him speaking to your heart.

- Discipline

  If you want intimacy with God, you must learn how to discipline and renew your mind through the Word of God, in prayer, and by worshipping the Lord. You can have a desire for intimacy with God, but without discipline in your life to create time for intimacy, it likely won't happen. We must make room for God in our lives. All the distractions of life that the enemy throws at us are designed to choke off our Father's life-giving breath, like weeds choke out a garden. Ask yourself, "Do I spend time creating an atmosphere where the Lord is welcome, or one where the enemy is welcome?" God desires fellowship with you. He is waiting.

- Delight

  You may have amazing times of worship at church or at conferences and events, but did you know that your greatest times of worship should take place when you are alone with your heavenly Father? God wants us to delight in Him. What do you delight in?

In what do you find the most pleasure? Make it your goal to delight in God's presence privately, more than you do publicly, and watch your relationship grow in deeper intimacy.

Dependency

I am convinced that there are a lot of people God cannot use simply because they live as though they "have it all together" without Him. Paul put it this way:

> Not many wise men according to the flesh, not many mighty men, and not many noble men were called. But God has chosen the foolish things of the world to confound the wise. God has chosen the weak things of the world to confound the things which are mighty. And God has chosen the base things of the world and things which are despised. Yes, and He chose things which did not exist to bring to nothing things that do, so that no flesh should boast in His presence.
>
> —1 Corinthians 1:26–29, mev

I don't know about you, but Paul's words describe me pretty well. There are many times when I feel like I have failed God miserably, when I don't feel very wise, or mighty or noble. In the eyes of the world, these things spell failure, but in the eyes of God, His strength is made perfect in our weakness (2 Cor. 12:9).

He is not calling the qualified; He is qualifying the called. He works best when we are totally dependent on Him. One of the greatest things God has worked in my life is a dependency upon Him. I used to think that I could handle anything, but I've learned that I do not have the answers without Him.

Jesus modeled dependency, and God's power flowed through His life. To the extent that you depend on yourself and what you can do, that's how much you defuse God's power in your life. Psalm 37:5 tells us to commit our way to the Lord and trust Him, and He will bring it to pass. When we are not dependent upon God, we are looking around for something or someone to depend upon, and the world is more than happy to give us ungodly things—our self, the economy, the government, our pastor, prophets. Jesus said, "I tell you the truth, the Son can do nothing by himself. He does only what he sees the Father doing" (John 5:19, NLT).

What things are getting in between you and a life of dependency upon God? Has Satan convinced you that you have what it takes to make it on your own? Is it time to check your dependency level?

Obedience

Jesus never once consulted His own will, never tried to please Himself. He only lived to do the will of the Father. Most of us do not understand that kind of obedience. He knew that the Father was engineering all the circumstances of His life, and we need to come to that understanding in our life if we are to embrace obedience as Jesus did. This is a revelation that will change the way you live, and it comes through intimacy. The greater your intimacy with the Lord, the greater your trust, and the greater your trust in the Lord, the greater your dependency, and the greater your dependency on Him, the greater your obedience.

Jesus could not live His life on His own, and He wanted His followers to understand that we cannot either. On the night before His crucifixion, Jesus gave His disciples "the keys of the kingdom of heaven," but Peter, not understanding what he was hearing, began to protest. Jesus, after rebuking Peter, begin to explain, saying, "If anyone desires to come after Me, let him deny himself, and take up his cross, and follow Me" (Matt. 16:24, NKJV).

Jesus knew He couldn't carry His cross on His own. That is what the cross does in each person's life—brings us to a breaking point where our own strength is no longer sufficient. I have come to this revelation personally, time and again, and each time I reach the same conclusion—I am no longer on the throne. He is on the throne, engineering all the circumstances of my life. On both the good days and the bad days, in the rough seasons and the calm times of life, God is in control. When my cross gets heavy, He is there to help carry it.

Make no mistake—God is working obedience in your life, and He will keep on working on you until your will lines up with His will, because He wants you to succeed. Paul wrote the following words of encouragement to the Philippian church: "Therefore, my beloved, as you have always obeyed, not as in my presence only, but now much more in my absence, work out your own salvation with fear and trembling; for it is God who works in you both to will and to do for His good pleasure" (Phil. 2:12–13, NKJV). The work of the cross purchased your salvation. Once God puts His will in you and begins to turn your will to want to do His pleasure, what He puts in, you have to work out. That is how you work out your salvation.

The enemy visited Jesus three times in the desert with three different temptations. Many scholars say those temptations were intended to be shortcuts to obeying the will of God. Jesus did not fall for it, and neither should you. Allow God to finish His work in you, to have complete control of your life, and in this way you will not fall prey to the devil and his evil schemes.

Press in to intimacy with God, in full dependency on Him, in obedience to His will. Stay connected to the source of all spiritual life; breathe in God's spirit and exhale His love in your life and to those around you.

Chapter Ten

THE POWER OF PRAYER

M Y MOTHER COMES from a very large family. Her mother died of a heart attack at the tender age of thirty-eight, just five days after giving birth to her eighteenth child. The task of caring for these children fell to my mother, who was only a child herself—just fourteen. Thankfully she had already developed a powerful prayer life. She would often go to pray in the family garden, where she had set up an old-fashioned altar. These private times of prayer sustained her.

At the age of twenty she was in the garden one day, praying, when she had a vision of a young man with black, wavy hair driving a green car. A few days later this man in the vision actually showed up at her doorstep! He was an evangelist preaching at a local revival. He remembered my mother from meeting her previously, and decided he wanted to see her again. He invited her to the revival, which she attended with her brother, and thus began their courtship and eventual marriage.

Mom knew that God was telling her something when she had the vision. She found the purpose, the plan, and the will of God for her life in her place of prayer—the garden. God wants to speak to you in your place of prayer, because He has a purpose, a plan, and a will for your life too.

Some of the most powerful people on the face of this earth are those who have learned how to pray. I'm not talking about people who merely believe in prayer, or talk about prayer, or those who can teach beautiful lessons on how to pray—but people who actually *take time to pray*. They take time away from other things, important and urgent things in their life, to seek God's counsel and wisdom.

I know we all have urgent "things" in life that vie for our attention on a daily basis, but the key to victorious living is to spend time with God first and urgent things second. Those things we think can't wait actually can wait. When you take the things of your life before God, He will give you heavenly strategies to deal with earthly things.

You have heard that prayer changes the atmosphere and shifts things in the spirit realm, and it does! It's true! In Paul's letter to the Thessalonian church he exhorted them to "pray without ceasing" (1 Thess. 5:17, MEV) because he knew that prayer is that holy communication with heaven that creates an atmosphere for God's presence.

The devil knows this too, and he will do whatever he can to distract you from your time of prayer. He knows that our greatest weapon is prayer. There is a Holy Ghost outpouring that happens when we pray that shakes the very foundations of hell. Earthquakes happen in the Spirit when we head to our place of prayer and get on our knees. Heaven and earth take notice because prayer is the power on earth that moves the power in heaven. Satan is not afraid of how long we shout. He is afraid of how deeply we pray.

If you are heading for your time and place of prayer with Abba Father and find yourself distracted by "urgent" things, or that need to check social media or TV, know that it's Satan trying to stop you from getting into that place of Holy Communion with God. Resist the devil, and he will flee from you! Hear the voice of God saying, "If you will, I will. If you will pray, I will act. If you will pray, I will move. If you will ask, I will answer. I will release My best into your life if you pray."

Prayer That Brings Victory

As believers we *must* learn to prevail in prayer. Everything that God wants to do is linked with prayer.

The holy men and women of God who subdue hell's threats are praying men and women, whose consistent, insistent, continual life of communication with God is not something they do, but a part of who they are. When prayer is part of what Christ means to you, you cannot separate it from who you are. It is this kind of prayer life that brings victory!

Prevailing prayer is not personal charisma. It is not programs, education, advertising, marketing, architectural design, or beautiful facilities. Without prayer, all of those things mean nothing. And prevailing prayer is not "foxhole praying" either. God has answered plenty of foxhole prayers, but the real shifting in the spiritual realm only comes from prevailing prayer.

Prevailing Prayer in the Old Testament

The Old Testament gives us examples of people who knew the power of prevailing prayer. Take Moses for instance. While he was meeting with God on Mt. Sinai, receiving the Ten Commandments, the people of Israel were building a golden calf-idol and corrupting themselves with drink and debauchery. God became angry and was ready to release His wrath, but Moses stood in the gap before God on behalf of the Israelites.

> And the LORD said to Moses, "I have seen this people, and indeed it is a stiff-necked people!

> Now therefore, let Me alone, that My wrath
> may burn hot against them and I may consume
> them. And I will make of you a great nation."
>
> —Exodus 32:9–10, NKJV

God was about to give Moses a promotion, but as for the rest, He was going to wipe the slate clean and start over. After spending time with God, Moses's great concern was for God's name and honor among the heathen nations. He was worried about what they would say about a God that wiped out His own people. So Moses put himself between the sinful people and the judgment of God, pleading on their behalf.

> Turn from your fierce anger; relent and do not
> bring disaster on your people. Remember your
> servants Abraham, Isaac and Israel, to whom
> you swore by your own self: "I will make your
> descendants as numerous as the stars in the sky
> and I will give your descendants all this land I
> promised them, and it will be their inheritance
> forever."
>
> —Exodus 32:12–13, NIV

It was the prevailing prayer of Moses that caused the Lord to relent from destroying the Israelites.

Then there was Joshua. God promised Joshua victory in battle, but the day began to slip away and still the battle raged in Gibeon. That's when Joshua went to the mat in prayer, calling for the sun to stand still over Gibeon until the Lord's purposes were accomplished (Josh. 10:12). God heard his prayer and answered, and time stood still until the battle was won!

In the Book of Isaiah we find Hezekiah prevailing in prayer. The King of Assyria was on the move, capturing all the fortified cities of Judah. Feeling emboldened, he sends a threatening letter to King Hezekiah, telling him that he was going to take Jerusalem also, because the God of Hezekiah will fail to deliver His people. Hezekiah responds in faith by going before the Lord. "It is true, LORD, that the Assyrian kings have laid waste all these peoples and their lands. They have thrown their gods into the fire and destroyed them, for they were not gods but only wood and stone, fashioned by human hands. Now, LORD our God, deliver us from his hand, so that all kingdoms of the earth may know that you, LORD, are the God." (Isa. 37:18–20). God's response: "Then the angel of the LORD went out and struck one hundred eighty-five thousand in the camp of the Assyrians. . . . So Sennacherib king of Assyria departed and returned home and lived in Nineveh" (Isa. 37:36–37, MEV). In Isaiah 38 Hezekiah became ill to the point of death. Again he cried out to God, who heard his prayer and granted him fifteen more years.

Prevailing Prayer in the New Testament

Jesus was well aware of the power of prayer, and the necessity of prevailing on your knees before the Father. In Matthew 17 Jesus illustrates how prevailing prayer can break the faith barrier. Most of you are very familiar with the story—Jesus and Peter, James, and John were returning from the mount of transfiguration, having just witnessed the glory of God in Jesus. As always a crowd gathers around Jesus. A desperate father makes his way through the crowd. His son has been afflicted by a demon of epilepsy since birth, and although he had taken the boy to some of Jesus's disciples, they were not able to help him. Kneeling down before Jesus, the father pleads for his son to be healed. Scripture tells us that, "Jesus rebuked the demon, and he came out of him. And the child was healed instantly" (Matt. 17:18, MEV).

But the disciples were confused. They didn't understand why Jesus had been able to cast out the demon and they couldn't. Jesus tells them: "Because of your unbelief. For truly I say to you, if you have faith as a grain of mustard seed, you will say to this mountain, 'Move from here to there,' and it will move. And nothing will be impossible for you. But this kind does not go out except by prayer and fasting" (vv. 20–21, MEV). In other words, sometimes you must prevail in prayer in order to break the faith barrier.

Although the disciples had enjoyed Jesus's presence, they had not yet learned to assimilate His power in their lives. And so it is with us. Often we get into God's presence, but it doesn't do anything for us in real life. We don't learn to draw from His presence and operate in His power and authority because we have not learned the importance of prevailing prayer. The man in Matthew 17 brought his son to the disciples with a plea of "help me." They tried, but they could not help because they were lacking time in prayer, lacking time in fasting—and lacking faith.

Once, when Jesus was returning from a time of private prayer, a disciple asked, "Lord, teach us to pray, as John also taught his disciples" (Luke 11:1, MEV). This request came from the heart of a man who had seen something precious. I wonder if he had perhaps followed Jesus to His secret prayer place and hid at a distance while the Lord prayed, watching and listening as the Son talked to the Father. What an unforgettable moment that would have been, as heaven's glory surrounded the Lord of lords. No wonder he wanted to be taught how to pray the same way—the way a son talks to a father.

> So He said to them, "When you pray, say: Our Father in heaven, hallowed be Your name. Your kingdom come. Your will be done on earth as

it is in heaven. Give us day by day our daily
bread. And forgive us our sins, for we also forgive everyone who is indebted to us. And do not
lead us into temptation, but deliver us from the
evil one."

—LUKE 11:2–4, NKJV

Then Jesus went on to tell them the parable of
the man knocking at his friend's door at midnight
to borrow some bread. "I say to you, though he will
not rise and give to him because he is his friend, yet
because of his persistence he will rise and give him as
many as he needs" (v. 8, NKJV). From this He explained:

Ask, and it will be given to you; seek, and you
will find; knock, and it will be opened to you.
For everyone who asks receives, and he who
seeks finds, and to him who knocks it will be
opened. If a son asks for bread from any of you
who is a father, will you give him a stone? Or if
he asks for a fish, will you give him a serpent
instead of a fish? Or if he asks for an egg, will
you offer him a scorpion? If you then, being evil,
know how to give good gifts to your children,
how much more will your heavenly Father give
the Holy Spirit to those who ask Him?

—LUKE 11:9–13, MEV

Matthew also recorded the Lord teaching them:

> Whatever you bind on earth will be bound in heaven, and whatever you loose on earth will be loosed in heaven.
>
> —MATTHEW 18:18, MEV

From these and other accounts in the Bible, God wants us to understand that prevailing prayer can win battles. It can add years to your life, conquer cancer, defeat heart disease, and cause a stroke to turn around and go back where it came from. Prevailing prayer brings victory! You can count on it.

STIR UP THE POWER OF PRAYER!

As believers we need to shake off the schemes of the devil and stir up the power of prayer in our lives! Are you concerned about a friend whose marriage is marked by violence? Prayer can get in where you cannot. Are there bad influences in your children's lives? Are there things coming against your marriage, your home, or your finances? Prayer goes to the middle of the situation and puts the devil in a headlock!

Sometimes it takes persistence before you see results. You may have found yourself in the midst of a struggle, and you pray and pray, yet it seems nothing changes. It has happened to me before. But then you decide to push harder and pray once more, and suddenly it is as if heaven breaks open and the victory is won!

The first-century New Testament church walked in amazing power, but sadly that is the opposite of what we often see in today's church. We need to restore the power and authority of God in the church, and it begins with prayer. Jesus taught the disciples that there is no distance in prayer, and there are no barriers on prayer. When we pray, we project ourselves—and His kingdom—into the situation. Our prayers can bind and loose authority; they can go where we cannot, imposing the will of God into the atmosphere. The only limit to prayer is how limited it is in our lives.

PATTERN AND PERSISTENCE

Jesus taught two important things about prayer: *pattern* and *persistence.* He constantly modeled these for His disciples, and His model is still available for us today.

Pattern

The Bible says that Jesus only did what His Father told Him to do. But how did He know what God wanted Him to do? He knew His Father's will because He had a habit of praying (Luke 5:16). How often do you make big decisions based solely on your experience and your wisdom? We think we can choose a spouse based on butterflies and emotions, but that isn't the blueprint Jesus gave us. The Son of God did nothing on His own without prayer.

After Jesus miraculously multiplied the bread and fish to feed five thousand people, He sent the disciples by boat across the Sea of Galilee to Gennesaret. Then, "He went up into the mountain by Himself to pray" (Matt. 14:23, MEV). He knew He couldn't walk on water, calm storms, and heal the masses without first dealing with them in the secret place of prayer.

When I read verses such as, "Now in the morning, having risen a long while before daylight, He went out and departed to a solitary place; and there He prayed" (Mark 1:35, NKJV), I like to say that Jesus was putting a deposit down so that He could write spiritual checks all day long. Too many of us try and write spiritual checks without making a prayer deposit, and guess what—they bounce all over the place because our account is empty. If you want to write spiritual checks all day, get up and pray before you go out of the house. Then you can speak to the mountain, and it will move. Then you can say, "Today I'll have good success, and I'll heal the sick. Today I can represent Christ." It all depends on making that deposit *first*, fighting the battles in prayer *first*. The only limit to prayer is how limited it is in our lives.

I've had people tell me, "I don't understand, Pastor. I prayed and nothing happened." The truth is, they commanded and spoke to the storm in the middle of the storm without making a deposit before the storm came. You will see victory when you live life storing up prevailing prayer. Then, when you stand in the storm, you know who you are and what authority you have.

Persistence

The only way to learn how to pray is to pray. Open your mouth and start saying things to God. Say exactly what you're feeling in your heart. Speak out loud. Prayer is not a quiet thing. That's why the devil wants to choke off our breath—because it takes breath to speak! Some of the most powerful praying you can do is when you speak back to God what He said to you through His Word.

Learn to pray the Word. Don't worry if you think you don't know how to do this. It's easy. Simply open the Bible and start praying the Word back to Him. Find His promises in His Word, and start saying them back to God. He loves it when we stand on His Word. Paul tells us, "Faith comes by hearing, and hearing by the word of God" (Rom. 10:17, MEV). Praying His Word back to Him builds faith, and faith energizes prayer.

In the Old Testament Daniel was a man of authority in prayer. There was war in the heavens, and Daniel was persistently praying and fasting for the restoration of Israel. Then he had an amazing visitation from an angel who told him, "Do not fear, Daniel, for from the first day that you set your heart to understand, and to humble yourself before your God, your words were heard; and I have come because of your words. But the prince of the kingdom of Persia withstood me twenty-one days" (Dan. 10:12–13, NKJV).

This is a very revealing passage. The angel is telling Daniel that God heard his request the first day he prayed it, but demonic forces battled against him, preventing him from answering Daniel's prayer right away. When a specific miracle has left the hand of God for you, the devil will fight to choke out your prayer life. It is persistent prayer that brings the breakthrough.

The very first day Daniel prayed, the answer to his prayer left the hand of God. I believe there are miracles that have already left the throne room, but are floating around in the spirit realm somewhere because we are not faithful to pray them in. Too often if we don't see the answer right away, we give up. That's when we need to press in, in faith. *Faith* says, "I will pray. I will knock. I will ask. I will seek until I get my deliverance." Jesus put it this way (notice there is no *sometimes* in this statement):

> For everyone who asks receives, and he who seeks finds, and to him who knocks, it will be opened.
>
> —MATTHEW 7:8, MEV

Chapter Eleven

PRAISE HIM!

OD'S WORD IS the language of praise. Deuteronomy 6:4–7 says, "Hear, O Israel: The LORD our God, the LORD is one! You shall love the LORD your God with all your heart, with all your soul, and with all your strength. And these words which I command you today shall be in your heart. You shall teach them diligently to your children, and shall talk of them when you sit in your house, when you walk by the way, when you lie down, and when you rise up" (NKJV).

God makes it very clear that His Word is what we are to teach our children, and yet I see the twenty-first-century church marrying the spirit of this age, and raising a generation of children who do not know the language of God or the language of the Holy Spirit. They have adopted the language of the culture instead of being taught the language of prayer and praise that pulls down strongholds. They are allowing the devil to silence the Word of God in their homes.

Nehemiah encountered this same issue in Jerusalem.

The people of God had broken the covenant of God and lost their language, and the city was nearly destroyed as a result. When Nehemiah arrived to begin rebuilding, only a small remnant remained. "In those days I also saw Jews who had married women of Ashdod, Ammon, and Moab. And half of their children spoke the language of Ashdod, and could not speak the language of Judah, but spoke according to the language of one or the other people" (Neh. 13:23–24, NKJV). When you read on, you see that Nehemiah was enraged by this discovery because the loss of the language meant the people of God were losing their culture. Men of God had married women who worshipped other gods, and the language of their children revealed the people's idolatry.

The same thing is happening in Christian homes today. There is a generation being raised that can't speak the spiritual language of our forefathers. The culture of our time has become their first language, and even those who are "bilingual" are speaking about the things of God merely as a *second* language. The Word of God is being choked out of family life because families are exposing themselves to more of the culture of the world than the culture of heaven. Children are learning to speak half Bible and half Oprah; half Word of God and half secular humanism; half living for Jesus and half living for the world. It's not enough to speak the language in church once a week. It must to be spoken fluently in the home if we expect our children to learn it and speak it. The next generation will never speak what we don't speak. We must speak God's Word in our homes every day so that it is the most familiar language our children hear and come to know. We cannot live God's life without limits outside His Word.

As always, Jesus is our model. He spoke only what He heard His Father speak. "For I have not spoken on My own authority, but the Father who sent Me gave Me a command, what I should say and what I should speak" (John 12:49, MEV). He knew the power of God's Word. That's how He resisted the devil in the wilderness. Every time the devil tried to tempt Him, Jesus responded with scripture. Now we have scripture *and* the blood of the Lamb to overcome the slings and arrows of the enemy. Revelation 12:11 tells us, "And they overcame him by the blood of the Lamb and by the word of their testimony, and they did not love their lives to the death" (NKJV). Stand firm, refusing to allow Satan to choke God's Word out of your house and your family. Let God's Word—the language of praise—be always on your lips.

PRAISE TO BRING HIS PRESENCE

When you raise your voice in praise, your ultimate goal should be to reach the presence of almighty God

Himself. Perhaps you are experiencing the glorious presence of God at church, but when you leave you don't take His presence with you. You return home "empty-handed" so to speak. As a pastor I am convinced that many of us are not taking God's presence home. We go to church and get happy, blessed, and excited, and then go home and let hell rule our family life. That may sound harsh, but I am afraid it is true for too many people.

If that sounds too familiar, then something is wrong, because whatever happens in the house of God should happen in your house as well. You cannot come to church on Sunday and then say "That was good, God, I enjoyed being in Your presence," and then cut Him off, exclude Him from your thoughts the rest of the week. When you live like God all week long, you will carry His presence with you wherever you go. One dose of God on Sunday is not enough. It will not carry you through. You need His presence 24/7, but how do you get His presence?

King David thought he knew how to get more of God's presence. In 1 Chronicles 13:9–14 we find the story of King David's attempt to bring God's presence back to His people, the Israelites. While David's intentions were good, he made the mistake of disrupting God's plan as to how the ark should be moved. If you recall, the ark was always to be carried upon the shoulders of men, but David decided to load it on an ox-drawn cart instead. When one of the oxen stumbled and the ark tipped to one side as if it were about to tumble off of the cart, one of David's men, named Uzza, put his hand on the ark to stabilize it. None of the holy things of God were to be touched upon penalty of death, and Uzza was immediately struck dead.

Upset and frightened, David decided not to bring the ark—the presence of God—home. Instead, he left it at the home of a humble man named Obed-Edom. Scripture says that, "The ark of God remained with the family of Obed-Edom in his house three months. And the LORD blessed the house of Obed-Edom and all that he had" (v. 14, NKJV).

We don't live in Old Covenant times. God's presence isn't contained in a box, and we won't be struck dead if we try and get close to God. Jesus died so that we now have access to God. The veil has been torn in two so that we can now come into God's presence all the time. God loves it when we come into His presence. He greatly desires that we draw close to Him, at all times, through worship, praise, and prayer, and in the way in which we live our lives every day. God doesn't want us to drawn close on Sunday only to draw away on Monday. He wants us to be close to Him every day, through a life of diligent praise and worship.

I believe God is saying to His people today, "It is

time for you to take Me home. I want to be in your
house. I want to bless you and all that you have. I want
to be in your marriage, on your job, on that plane with
you, and in that car with you. I do not want you to
leave My presence and cut Me off from your personal
life; I want you to receive blessings at home. I want to
visit you in intimate ways when you are alone."

Obed-Edom was not a king. He was not a mighty
man. In fact, he was not even a soldier. His name does
not appear anywhere else in the Bible. But he desired
the presence of God. When he saw that the king did
not want God's presence in his home, Obed-Edom
said, "I'll take it," and the Bible states that the ark of
the covenant was placed in his care. I researched the
name Obed-Edom and found that one of its meanings
is *worshipper.* I believe worship and prayer were constant in Obed-Edom's house. If you desire to maintain
the presence of God in your home, a certain attitude must be present—you have to desire His presence. Obed-Edom had to rearrange his priorities. He
had to be the high priest in his home and take control of what took place in his home if he wanted God's
presence to remain. He had eight sons, and not one of
them was backslidden, not one was on drugs, not one
was in prison or living in sin. The Bible says all eight
of them were mighty men of valor.

When we bring the presence of God home, our

family will be impacted—our children and our marriage will be affected. When we bring God home, the atmosphere of our lives will be changed, and peace and contentment will prevail. Invite Him home today. Let your praise and worship create a place in your heart and in your home for the presence of almighty God, and watch His blessings flow. Praise Him in the morning, praise Him at noontime, praise Him in the evening—just praise Him!

Be a Rainmaker

We don't need look far in this beautiful country of ours to see that there is a great deal of spiritual dryness. America desperately needs the rain of the Holy Spirit. Our churches need rain, our families need rain, our neighborhoods, cities, and states need rain—and that will only happen when prayer and praise change the atmosphere. God wants you to be a rainmaker. Praise and worship are the language of heaven, and they will unleash God's Holy Spirit on our dry places. There's a simple principle at work here—no worship and praise, no rain.

This principle is illustrated in the Book of Zechariah, and it is one of the greatest lessons the Lord ever taught me about worship. It changed my life. "And it will happen that if any of the families of the earth do not go up to Jerusalem to worship the King, the LORD of Hosts, then there will not be rain for them" (Zech. 14:17, MEV). No worship, no rain, it's that simple. Praise is like a cloud that forms in the atmosphere. Once enough of it accumulates, it drops rain.

Psalm 150:6 says everything that has breath should praise the Lord. We are designed by God to praise Him, but so often our churches don't encourage real praise. Worship can seem dry and lifeless, but it doesn't have to be. We can invite the Holy Spirit into our worship. He will energize us with the joy of heaven. Worship isn't about singing for people; it is all about singing for the King of kings, for the King of glory Himself! Next time you worship, invite the Holy Spirit in. Kick in and get your praise on! Open up your heart to our matchless King Jesus and let the praise in your heart flow to His throne.

There are many expressions of praise to be found in the Bible. One is simply the lifting of your hands: "Lift up your hands in the sanctuary and praise the LORD" (Ps. 134:2, NIV). Lifting our hands is scriptural and a unique expression of praise. Your fingerprints distinguish you from everyone else. When you raise them to God, I believe you are reaching out and touching Him in a way that symbolizes your unique individual relationship with Him. And that is what God desires— relationship with us.

Scripture also tells us to clap our hands and shout to God (Ps. 47:1). A shout can change a "dry" atmosphere. I have been in many services when the songs of praise were going just so high. Then someone full of praise shouts out, "Hallelujah! Praise the Lord!" and the whole place breaks loose with shouts and songs of praise. Psalm 150:4 tells us to praise the Lord with dance, leaping, bowing down before Him, and even by standing to your feet in honor of His presence. Whichever way you choose to praise Him, your praise changes the atmosphere and breaks the grip of the enemy off your life because it strengthens your relationship with the Father.

David was a warrior, but he was first and foremost *a worshipper*. He played music and sang praises to the Lord from the time he was a child. His praise was a powerful weapon against the enemy. When David played his harp for King Saul, the "distressing spirit" that tormented Saul was subdued (1 Sam. 16:23, NKJV). Likewise, every time you pluck a guitar, hit a chord, beat a drum, crash a cymbal or raise your voice in praise to God, you send the devil running out and loose the rain of the Holy Spirit into the atmosphere.

MIDNIGHT HOUR PRAISE

There is power in our praise because it is connected to the victory Jesus won over the devil and everything he has put in motion against us. In 2 Chronicles

20 we find a large army coming to make war against Jehoshaphat. When he received the news, Jehoshaphat and the people of Judah sought the Lord through fasting and prayer. Everyone gathered, and Jehoshaphat prayed, seeking help from God and waiting upon Him. Then they bowed in worship before the Lord and began to sing and praise Him loudly. The next day Jehoshaphat put the praisers and worshippers in *front* of the army. When the enemy armies heard the praise, they turned on each other and destroyed themselves.

We need to base our praise on who Jesus is, not on our circumstances. Paul and Silas were not just "sunshine praisers" who worshipped God only when things were going well. They were midnight, dirty-dungeon praisers as well. Perhaps Paul didn't have the greatest singing voice, but things like that don't matter to God. He is interested in our hearts, our character. I think God loves it when someone who is in his or her midnight hour still has praise.

We don't walk out and celebrate publicly what we haven't celebrated privately. The greater your private worship, the greater your public ministry will be. What you do all week in private will determine your anointing in public. Constant private worship equals powerful public worship. If Paul and Silas had languished in that cell focusing on how badly they were treated, how they felt defeated, or how they would get even with those who beat them, they would have rotted in that cell. When the devil blocks our praise, our breakthrough gets blocked, and our victory gets locked up. You'll never experience victory as long as you are talking defeat.

If you have breath, you can praise the Lord. You may not have a job, but you have breath. You may not have a car, but you have breath. His Word says that He tests us in the furnace of affliction (Isa. 48:10). Perhaps you are in the midst of a fiery furnace with your health or in your marriage or family. If that's you, then it's time to ramp up the praise. Praise will lift your spirit out of the depths, and when your spirit soars, the rest of you will follow. I believe God greatly values praise that is borne out of our times of adversity or affliction. There is a particular sound of worship that can only come from one who has gone through trials. When you go through the fire, you can see what you really have inside.

As I said earlier, there are many ways to praise the Lord—with lifted hands, dancing feet, and bowed bodies. But there is a praise that needs nothing but your breath. It is a praise that rises out of the furnace where you have lost everything *but* your breath. It is a praise that is not attached to material possessions or specific happenings. It is a praise that comes when you praise God in spite of it all. A heart after God finds a way to praise Him, even in the heat of the trial. Set your heart on God who is faithful, who loves you, who has called you and equipped you to overcome. Determine that as long as you have breath, you will praise Him.

Sometime ago I read a story about a fire that started in a computer store in South Bend, Indiana. The local fire department was first on the scene. They hosed the outside of the building, but it was having little effect on the fire inside. As the fire continued to spread and become more intense, they sent out a call for assistance from other fire companies. One of the smaller departments from a neighboring county rushed to help. They had a small budget, and their fire truck was old. When they arrived at full speed, they went right over the curb, across the yard, and right through the wall of the building into the fire. While they were in there, they pulled their water hoses out and went to work. They managed to put out the fire that couldn't be handled before. They were able to do more from the inside than the other fire company could do from the outside.

The next day the owner of the business offered that little fire company a check for ten thousand dollars in appreciation for the bravery they showed by driving right into the middle of the fire. When the press asked the fire chief what he would use the money for, he told them the first thing they would do is buy some new brakes for their truck! Those firemen never planned to go straight into the middle of the fire. Maybe you didn't plan to be where you are right now. God wants you to know that He has you there because there are things you can do from the inside of that fiery situation better than you can do from the outside. You can't tell how powerful your faith is until you've been into the fire. God wants to unlock your praise. It can be your response no matter what you face.

When I was a kid, we spent a lot of time playing on the neighborhood playground. We had team captains who were always the bigger, stronger guys. They would divide up the rest of us kids one by one as they chose team members. It could be embarrassing for little guys like me to be left standing there thinking, "Please, God, don't let me be last." In life there's always somebody who is picked last, someone who doesn't seem qualified to be on the team, but not so with God. What qualifies us for God's team is often the furnace. If you are in a furnace, take heart! It is an indication that God has an assignment for you.

Think about the men of God in the Bible. Joseph, for instance—he was chosen out of the fire. Despised by his own family, rejected, tempted, lied about, falsely accused, and punished for a crime he did not commit, yet in the end Joseph knew that what men meant for evil, God would use for good. God chose Joseph out of the fire, put him in a palace, and used him to save a generation.

And what about David—he too was chosen out of the fire. He didn't try and deny that trouble existed, but he knew God was the deliverer no matter what happened. In Psalm 34:19 David said, "The righteous person has many troubles, but the LORD rescues him from all of them" (GW).

And then there was Job. If ever someone was chosen out of the fire, it was Job. He was a man determined to serve God no matter what. He lost everything—his children, his livelihood, his wealth, his health. He had nothing left but his breath, and with his breath he praised God. "Though He slay me, yet will I trust Him" (Job 13:15, NKJV). "When He has tested me, I shall come forth as gold" (Job 23:10, NKJV).

Some think we are formed and made in the fiery furnace of adversity, but what really happens in that furnace is that it reveals who we are, what we are made of on the inside. As believers, we need only to tap into the unlimited resources of the One who lives within us in the midst of adversity. He is our portion and our cup, and there is always enough with Jesus.

POSITIONED FOR VICTORY

It's a good thing God sees more in us than we see in ourselves. Take Gideon for example. He was an ordinary guy from the smallest tribe of Israel yet God used him to defeat an entire army. As the story unfolds, we find Gideon hiding in a winepress. The Israelites had fallen into sin, worshipping the demon gods of the Amorites. Things kept going from bad to worse until God finally turned them over to their enemy, the Midianites. Life under the Midianites was so bad that the Israelites were forced to flee to the mountains and caves. Still the Midianites followed them, ravaging their land and destroying their crops and livestock. Finally, in desperation, God's people cried out to Him, and God answered them, in a very unlikely way—with an ordinary man found hiding in a winepress.

> The LORD turned to him and said, "Go in the strength you have and save Israel out of Midian's hand. Am I not sending you?" "Pardon me, my lord," Gideon replied, "but how can I save Israel? My clan is the weakest in Manasseh, and I am the least in my family." The LORD answered, "I will be with you, and you will strike down all the Midianites, leaving none alive." Gideon replied, "If now I have found favor in your eyes, give me a sign that it is really you talking to me. Please do not go away until I come back and bring my offering and set it before you." And the LORD said, "I will wait until you return."
> —JUDGES 6:14–18, NIV

As the rest of the story unfolds, we find Gideon accomplishing the seemingly impossible. First he tears down his father's altars to the demon gods of the Amorites. Then, with just three hundred men, he defeats the Midianite army. You will recall that the Midianite army was camped out for the night in the valley. To build Gideon's confidence, the Lord told him to go down to the enemy's camp and listen to what was being said. So Gideon took a buddy down the hill with him. They carefully made their way to one of the tents. Why would God tell Gideon to go listen in the middle of the night when the enemy should have been sound asleep? Simple: the tables had turned, and it was time for the enemy to have nightmares.

One soldier woke up his tent mate to tell him about a dream he had. "'A round loaf of barley bread came tumbling into the Midianite camp. It struck the tent with such force that the tent overturned and collapsed.' His friend responded, 'This can be nothing other than the sword of Gideon son of Joash, the Israelite. God has given the Midianites and the whole camp into his hands'" (Judg. 7:13–14, NIV).

Do you see what is happening here? We should not be the ones tossing and turning all night, filled with fear and anxiety. When the people of God are worried, the wrong camp is worried. We need to cause a nightmare in the camp of the enemy.

The story continues with Gideon returning to his small band of three hundred soldiers. Giving each one a trumpet, an empty pitcher, and a torch to hide under the pitcher, he divides them into three groups and they proceed to surround the camp of the enemy on three sides. "Then the three companies blew the trumpets and broke the pitchers—they held the torches in their left hands and the trumpets in their right hands for blowing—and they cried, 'The sword of the LORD and of Gideon!'" (Judg. 7:20, NKJV). All of this caused such fear and confusion in the enemy's camp that they turned on each other, killing one another as they fled. The victory belonged to God and His people, and it still does!

God took an ordinary man who did not see himself as brave or valiant, and used him in a mighty way. You are equipped to cause nightmares for the enemy. Just like Gideon, God will call you to move past those things in your life that seem too big to defeat so that you can walk in the destiny He has planned for you. Gideon didn't realize it, but God had already given him the victory (Judg. 6:16). All Gideon had to do was walk out and express that victory.

As God's people we have been positioned for victory through the death and the resurrection of Jesus Christ. We have been positioned to turn hell into pandemonium. It is time to say, "Enough of the 'demon'-strations! Now is the time for a clear demonstration of God's anointing in the life of every believer that will shake the gates of hell off their hinges! God promises to be with us. He is our refuge and our strength, a very present help in times of trouble. He will bring the victory, every time, if we trust Him.

TRADE INDEPENDENCE FOR GOD-DEPENDENCE

One of the three "weapons" of Gideon's army was broken clay pitchers, because God knows that one of the greatest threats to the enemy is a broken vessel. It was those broken clay vessels God used that helped defeat the enemy. It is not your strength but your brokenness that God uses. It is not your gift but your yieldedness; not your independence but your dependence on Him that prevails.

Paul and Silas were arrested and thrown into prison, and revival broke out. They were beaten and left to rot, but at midnight the two began to pray and praise God, because if they couldn't sleep, neither would the devil. Paul started singing, Silas joined in and God's voice made it a trio, and that old jailhouse started to tremble. If your problems are keeping you up at night, it is time to start keeping the devil up with your praise.

We need to understand our identity in Christ, who we are in Christ. We are not limited by the devil. We are made to live life without limits by the One who lives in us. We have all power in the name of Jesus, against sickness, disease, lack, and fear. We are broken vessels, but when we yield our brokenness to God, His strength is made perfect in our weakness (2 Cor. 12:9).

Wield the Weapon of Praise

Let's take a moment to look at some of the characteristics of praise.

Praise is a weapon.

Some things will not break loose until you shout a good "Hallelujah." Praise is a weapon. It brings victory. It brings deliverance. It helps to make a way where there is no way.

Praise activates the spirit world.

Rock groups understand that music activates the spirit world, and demons are activated by demonic music. We need to realize that singing praise to God also activates angels, which are called "ministering spirits" (Heb. 1:14, MEV).

Praise is a lifestyle.

Praise is something you do every day. Praise is something with which you fill your mind all week long. You have to live a life of praise if you want to loose the deadly grip of the devil.

Praise frees others.

When we begin to praise God in spirit and in truth, other people are listening and may be blessed. When Paul and Silas praised and the earthquake brought deliverance, "everyone's chains were loosed" (Acts 16:26, NKJV). When you praise the Lord in your house, you create an atmosphere where deliverance can come to everybody around you.

Praise must be wholehearted.

If you want to get a release of God's power in your life, you can't be halfhearted about your commitment to God by serving Him halfway; you have to go all the way. You can't get the blessing if you're only half-changed or you only offer Him halfhearted praise. The key is to go all the way with God.

Praise is often simply recounting the faithfulness and greatness of God in times past.

We frequently see David and other Old Testament writers reminding the people of God to remember His faithful, wondrous acts.

Praise confounds the enemy and releases the power of God.

In 2 Kings 3 we find the story about two kings—Jehoram, king of Israel, and Jehoshaphat, king of Judah. These two kings joined forces to defeat the king of Moab, but unfortunately they found themselves in big trouble even before the battle began—they had miscalculated the amount of water they needed for the journey. When they realized their predicament, they thought the Lord had sentenced them to death. Finally, after much gnashing of teeth, they thought it might be good to seek the counsel of the Lord, so they asked for a prophet. When they found out Elisha was nearby, they went and found him.

Now, as you may recall, Elisha had a double portion of Elijah's anointing. He had miracle power. He was a man who had left everything to follow the call of God. So there he is, eager to serve the Lord, and along comes the king of Israel and the king of Judah along with the king of Edom, whose land they were crossing. Elisha knew of the sins of Jehoram and was none too happy about it. He wasn't going to seek the Lord on behalf of a sinning king who had no fear or love of God in his heart.

When Jehoram approached him for counsel, Elisha told him to go consult Ahab and Jezebel, the idol-worshipping prophets of his parents. Concerned that the Lord had given the victory to the enemy, Jehoram pleaded further. Finally Elisha responded, "As the LORD of hosts lives, before whom I stand, surely *were it not that I regard the presence of Jehoshaphat king of Judah*, I would not look at you, nor see you. But now bring me a musician" (vv. 14–15, NKJV, emphasis added).

But Jehoshaphat, he was a different story. He was the king of Judah, and the name *Judah* means *Jehovah be praised.* Jehoram may not have done anything right up to this point, except for bringing Jehoshaphat. At the sight of Jehoshaphat, Elisha called for some praise music, because he knew he needed to invite the presence of the Lord into the situation. As the musician played, the Word of the Lord came to Elisha:

> "Make this valley full of ditches." For thus says the LORD: "You shall not see wind, nor shall you see rain; yet that valley shall be filled with water, so that you, your cattle, and your animals may drink." And this is a simple matter in the sight of the LORD; He will also deliver the Moabites into your hand.
>
> —2 KINGS 3:16–18, NKJV

Elisha clearly says in verse 14, "If it had not been for praise in this room, I would not even look at you. I would not even listen to you. I would not even give you the time of day. If it were not for the presence of praise in this room, I would just walk out and leave you on your own to get out of this mess." Elisha was saying that when you get in trouble, it takes praise to deliver you. Nothing else would have gotten Jehoram out of this situation.

I believe there are many lost souls who would still be bound up and held hostage by the devil had it not been for praise. I believe there are a lot of sicknesses that would still be on people had it not been for praise. I believe a lot of people would still be held by the throes of depression or addiction if it were not for praise. God wants you to become familiar with praise. He wants you to learn how to wield it as a weapon of warfare, because there is power in praise. He wants to hear your praises rise as incense to His throne.

Occupy the Valley With Praise

We all enjoy sharing our "mountaintop" experiences—those times with God when He heals our hearts, restores our strength, and His love lifts us out of the mud and mire. We tend not to talk as much about our "valley" experiences, but I want to change your opinion about valleys.

In 1 Samuel 17 the Philistine army had come to make war against the army of Israel. The Philistines stood on one mountain, and Israel stood on another mountain with a valley in between them (v. 3). Now Goliath, the champion of the Philistines, stood about nine feet tall and carried a huge shield and a fourteen-foot spear, and went about scaring the bejeebers out of the Israelites. Every day for forty days he would walk down into that valley to defy God and taunt the army of Israel. Forty is the number for testing, and Israel was failing the test. Goliath was the first thing they heard in the morning and the last thing they heard at night. Day after day the taunting voice of the enemy and all of his threats would rain down on their ears, eroding their confidence. Just as with Gideon, the wrong camp was intimidated. The Israelite army tossed and turned at night with the threats of Goliath echoing in their minds.

Did you know that whatever dominates your mind in the morning and evening will likely establish what kind of life you are going to have? If you go to bed worried and wake up worried, chances are you're going to have a worried day. Goliath sent the Israelites to bed worried and woke them up worried. He wanted to occupy the valley, but problem was, he didn't own the valley. The valley belonged to Judah—it belonged to praise! It's the same in your life. Your valley doesn't belong to fear, it doesn't belong to worry, it doesn't belong to the devil. It belongs to praise.

Then along came a young shepherd boy from Bethlehem named David, bringing food for his brothers in the army. Now David was a worshipper. He learned how to worship as a shepherd tending his sheep. Every night and every morning in the fields his thoughts would be filled with praise to God. So when he arrived and heard the defiant rants of the enemy, he couldn't believe the mighty army of Israel was just "taking it" and doing nothing. David went to King Saul and said, "Let me go fight Goliath, because one day I was watching my sheep, and a lion attacked, and I snatched the lamb out of the lion's mouth and slew the lion. Another day a bear attacked, and I killed it with my bare hands. I learned through praise how powerful my God is!"

We all know how the story ends; it's one of the most well known in the Bible. But I want you to understand one thing: David faced Goliath with praise on his lips. He ran toward Goliath with a determination that his enemy would not be victorious in that valley. You don't have to deny the darkness of the valley when those seasons come along, but you don't have to turn the valley over to the enemy either. Life is full of real issues, real hardships, but praise is real too, and it's powerful; more powerful than any issue you might face, because praise harnesses the power of heaven.

In the story of David and Goliath the real battle was not between David and Goliath. The real battle was about who was going to occupy the valley. And that's the real battle in our lives too—who is going to occupy your valley? You or your enemy? Fear or praise? A young, praise-filled shepherd boy ran toward Goliath, loaded his sling, and let the river rock fly. He made a final, lasting "impression" on Goliath and dropped him where he stood. In that moment rightful owner-ship of the valley was restored. The power of fear gave way to the power of praise.

One thing that I really appreciate about David is the fact that he was not always happy. He suffered through difficult seasons in his life just as we do. He was rid-iculed and rejected by his older brothers. King Saul hunted him and repeatedly tried to kill him. His own children turned on him in his old age, attempting to take the throne. Like you and me, David was someone who endured the full range of emotions that life can bring. And just like you and me, David had to learn how to be victorious in tough seasons.

Perhaps you have taken an amazing vacation that you just couldn't stop raving about when you returned to work. Your coworkers hear you talking about it and want to know more, and you are more than happy to share every detail with anyone who will listen. Some even say they might book a vacation to the same spot next year. Your praise caused others to want to know more. The same is true of the Lord. Psalm 76:1 reads, "In Judah God is known; His name is great in Israel" (NKJV). As I mentioned earlier, Judah means *praise*. We come to know God in praise, and when we praise Him, we make Him known to others.

You may be in the toughest season of your life right

now. Bad times do come to good people. We will always be faced with seasons of attack. God wants you to understand that you do not come to know Him through mere mental ascension. You come to know Him and all that He can do through worship and praise, and it is there in that place of praise that He will break the strongholds in your life.

God wants you to fill the mountaintops and the valleys in your life with praise. He wants you to take praise onto your battlefields, into your church, to work, into your home. He wants you to walk away from just reading about praise and walk into a lifestyle of praise so that you can have victory in every area of your life, so that when the battle rages, you aren't overcome by fear, but it is you who overcomes fear with praise!

Chapter Twelve

HAVE FAITH!

PERFECT LOVE IS love without an agenda, love that forgives. When you move into that realm of perfect love, you enter into what Jesus entered into when He went to the cross. The last thing Jesus said before He died was, "Father, forgive them." That kind of love is the highest level of faith. The number-one thing that makes your faith work is not just your confession—and I believe in confession. The highest level of faith is love. We don't have to wrestle with the gates of hell. We have the keys to the gates, but we must break through to the highest level of faith to use them. We need to break the prayer barrier and move in faith into perfect love.

If those keys will work on the gates of hell, they will work anywhere. They are the keys to financial blessings, the keys to miracles and healing, and the keys to signs and wonders in the church, because when the church moves in love, miracles start happening. Are you really trying to accommodate what God wants to do in the church? We read about revival overseas, but are we ready to go to a level of perfect love where we can see it in the church in America?

There are multilevels of faith, and our faith grows as we grow in God. You may hit barriers in your faith walk, but don't let that discourage you. Barriers can be broken. You can go as high as you believe God can take you. In his letter to the Romans, Paul said, "The righteousness of God is revealed from faith to faith; as it is written, 'The just shall live by faith'" (Rom. 1:17, NKJV). In 2 Thessalonians 1:3 Paul again talks about faith: "Your faith grows exceedingly, and the love of every one of you all abounds toward each other" (NKJV).

Faith, one of the fruits of the Spirit, starts out small, like a seed. Over time the seed of faith grows until there is fruit, but this process takes time. A tree starts with a seed that grows and eventually results in a tree. Then the tree produces a bloom that fades to reveal immature fruit. The tree nurtures its immature fruit until it reaches maturity and ripens. Our faith is a lot like a tree, needing to grow and be constantly fed, nurtured and cultivated in order to produce fruit. Galatians 5:6 speaks of the highest level of faith: "The only thing that counts is faith expressing itself through love" (NIV). Faith works by love, and the highest level of faith is *perfect love*. God wants each one of us to allow His Holy Spirit to grow and nurture our faith so that we might offer the fruit of His perfect love to a hurting world.

Many years ago our church experienced a period of explosive growth. Denominational and racial barriers were being torn down for the first time in our small, Southern community. In short God was "pouring out His Spirit upon all flesh," and our congregation represented that outpouring. We were growing by the hundreds, and it was hard not to notice what God was doing. The more we grew, the more prominent we became in our community. We became "the talk of the town." With all this growth, our youth program grew too, and it became apparent that we needed to expand our facility to accommodate the needs of the young people. We embarked on a building program with the goal of building a $3 million youth and media center. With over $900,000 in savings, we were able to approached a local bank and secure a loan for the remainder of the money. With what seemed like a "green light" we forged ahead with our building program, unaware of how much our faith would be tested in the coming months.

As construction progressed, we eventually exhausted our cash reserves. When we went to the bank to make the first withdrawal on our secured loan, to our great surprise, the bank and its board of directors refused to give us the money, with no explanation. I asked for a meeting with the president of the bank. At that meeting I was told that they had changed their minds and were no longer interested in being part of our church's growth. I was perplexed and shocked. We had impeccable credit. We were a blessing to our community through many outreaches. What would we do? The building project was in full swing, the steel beams were up, but we suddenly had no more money to draw upon.

Looking back, I realized that the bank's behavior was an attack from the enemy to try and prevent our church from reaching more souls for the kingdom. There were some in our community who were not fans of our church and didn't like the fact that a "Spirit-filled church" was growing. In praying and fasting for revival, we were seeing many saved and filled with the Holy Spirit. During this time period we even broke out into a five-week revival with evangelist Perry Stone. Spiritually we had attracted the attention of the spirit of the enemy.

I told the bank president in our meeting that if they didn't keep their word and give us the money as promised for the loan, I would inform our congregation of their actions. He grinned and smugly said, "Do what you like, but we will not change our minds." That Sunday morning I got up and shared my heavy heart with our congregation. It felt like our vision to reach our city, state, and nation was stopped in its tracks.

Our media department, our offices, and many out-
reach ministries were to be in that building as well. I
shared the bad news, and then I challenged them to
do what I was going to do—I was going to remove my
personal bank account from that bank.

That same evening an elderly, trusted minister
named E. L. Terry came to our church and shared
that God had told him that what had happened with
the bank would turn out for our good. He said that
we would not need the loan because God was going
to bless Free Chapel so that we could build the new
building and be debt free. After his words the church
exploded into thunderous applause.

The next morning the parking lot of the bank was
full. Inside there were nine or ten customers in each
line saying, "I'm from Free Chapel and will be closing
my account." By noon I received a call asking me to
attend an emergency meeting the bank had called
with its board. When I arrived, they presented a con-
tract for the loan and said "Preacher, you have just
about ruined our bank." That was when I informed
the president of the bank, along with the board members in attendance, that we would no longer need the
loan—we were going to trust God. Later I learned that
more than five million dollars had been withdrawn
from the bank that day.

I don't have any explanation for what happened over

the next few months. All I know is that every week we would tell the church how much we needed financially, and every week for almost a year we met that need miraculously. Some weeks we needed $350,000 or more above our operating expenses to pay the bills, and every week God supplied the need. God broke the enemy's grip on our finances and our faith. We moved into our new building debt free for the glory of God.

My prayer for you is that your faith will grow and increase so that you are able to do *all* that God calls you to do. What God did for us, He will do for you too. The power of your faith will break the devil's grip on your finances and your life because "Greater is He who is in you than he who is in the world" (1 John 4:4, NAS).

GO BEYOND POSITIVE THINKING

I believe God is looking for people who will dare to break out of comfortable places and say, "I'm going to another level." If you are going to walk in faith, if you are going to break the barrier and move into a new dimension, it will be because you take risks, because you determine not to become satisfied, because you make a conscious decision to push on to greater things.

I remember one time I was praying and I sensed God telling me, "I do not need another motivational preacher." Those words really caused me to stop and think about things for a while. I realized that although there is a place in the body of Christ for those who encourage, motivate, and coach others, God was not calling me to that place. He wasn't calling me to be a life coach or a motivational speaker. God was calling me to preach fiery, Spirit-filled messages and pray fiery, Spirit-filled prayers! He has called me to raise up a remnant of sold-out Christians who live life in light of eternity.

In this great spiritual battle all believers are engaged in, God has given us spiritual weapons that go beyond positive thinking. Paul said we are "mighty in God for pulling down strongholds, casting down arguments and every high thing that exalts itself against the knowledge of God, bringing every thought into captivity to the obedience of Christ, and being ready to punish all disobedience when your obedience is fulfilled" (2 Cor. 10:4–6, NKJV). What that means is, I can't "coach" the devil out of your life because it takes more than positive thinking or motivational speeches to break free from the grip of the enemy. It takes spiritual warfare to break Satan's grip. We must get into a place where we have zero tolerance for sin in our lives, zero tolerance for distractions and any other thing that opens the door to Satan and his minions. Each one of us must learn how to take a bold stand in the authority of Christ, through faith and prayer and praise. Faith will rise in you when we pray and seek holiness until sin becomes exceedingly sinful to you.

Isaiah 59:19 promised, "When the enemy comes in like a flood, the Spirit of the LORD will lift up a standard against him" (NKJV). Are you leaving your floodgates open through prayerlessness? Don't do it! Is your faith level at low ebb? Learn to live an obedient, prayerful life, and your level of consecration will rise along with your faith. The less sin you tolerate in your life, the higher your standards of righteousness, the more power you'll have to tear down and take captive to the obedience of Christ every lofty thing that exalts itself against the knowledge of God.

It's time to break the faith barrier in your life. Elijah was a man who broke the faith barrier. He boldly proclaimed to the wicked, idolatrous leadership of Israel that there would be no rain in the land, that the rain would cease and begin at his word (1 Kings 17:1). After three years of drought the Word of God finally came to Elijah. He told Ahab to go eat and drink because he could hear "the sound of abundance of rain" (1 Kings 18:41, NKJV). Then Elijah went up to the top of Mt. Carmel, bowed down, and told his servant to go and look toward the sea. His servant looked but saw nothing. Seven times Elijah sent him back to look again. Seven times the servant obeyed. Finally, the last time, he came back and reported with excitement,

"There is a cloud, as small as a man's hand, rising out of the sea!" (v. 44, NKJV). The clouds rolled in and the rain came down, just as Elijah said.

Elijah had persistence. He had the kind of faith that reaches up and grabs nothing until it becomes something. He had the kind of faith that grabs hold of a promise in the heavenlies and will not let go until it manifested in his life. Elijah went from just knowing God's Word to moving in the reality of it, *by faith*. It is one thing to know the Word, proclaim the Word, and preach the Word. It is one thing to talk about healing, talk about miracles, talk about salvation, or talk about household blessing, but I want to *see these things take place!* It is time for a faith breakthrough. We need to share the gospel *and* demonstrate it as well, in the power of the Holy Spirit, remembering Paul's words—that his preaching was not "persuasive words of human wisdom," but a demonstration of the Spirit's power (1 Cor. 2:4, NKJV).

PRESS ON TO NEW LEVELS

God wants you to break some faith barriers and go deeper, to get you to that place where you tap into something you can't get over, something that radically changes your life, until you start flowing with it because you can't control it. The Holy Spirit of God goes in whatever direction He wants to go, and He invites you along for the amazing ride of faith. Whatever God wants to do, you should be willing to yield and bend to His perfect will. If you seriously go with God, you will not stay where you are, nor will you go back to the past because God intends you to break through. He wants you to move into a new dimension, into the highest level of faith. He wants you to press on until you reach that perfect love realm where faith works.

How many times do you get to the point where all you need to do is just press through the difficulty you are facing to get to the next level, but instead of pressing in, you become fearful, or too comfortable, and back up instead of going forward? There is something to be learned from the Prophet Ezekiel in this regard. He had an interesting encounter with an angel of the Lord. "Then he brought me back to the door of the temple; and there was water, flowing from under the threshold of the temple toward the east" (Ezek. 47:1, NKJV). Now, most people when they read this, they focus on the river flowing *from* the temple, but I want you to notice that Scripture says the angel of the Lord brought him *back* to that door. That means Ezekiel had been at the door before.

Maybe it's time to ask yourself a question? Does God keep bringing you back to the door over and over again? Remember, He will bring you to it, but He will not push you through it. Only your faith can break the barrier and take you to the next level. It's time to get excited because just on the other side of that door is an exciting new season about to break loose in your life! God wants you to break through because otherwise He'll keep bringing you back to that door over and over again. Don't give up! Press on to the next level with God. He is with you! Be that part of the church that is willing to change from audience to army. Catch the wind of the Holy Spirit and be a "gone with the wind" kind of believer who operates at a new level of faith, where your chains are gone and the wind of the Spirit is propelling you from glory to glory in a life lived without limits.

Make Your Plans Large

Do you realize that God has already spoken your destiny over you? That's why the devil tries so hard to distract you and steer you away from God. None of us will ever reach our full God-given potential as long as we remain small on the inside. In order to grow to God's full potential, you must have faith to let God increase your capacity through journeys of faith and trusting Him because He is a God of maximum capacity. Whatever you are believing Him for, believe Him for the maximum and watch Him enlarge your capacity. When Jesus told the disciples to throw their nest over the other side of the boat and they would pull in a great harvest, they couldn't understand what He was saying. They were seasoned fisherman, but in faith they did what Jesus said and the result was a miraculous catch.

Jesus wants you to have the same kind of faith. He may tell you to throw your net over the other side of the boat, and when He does, do it! Have faith! God wants to do so much more than you are asking and believing Him for right now. Paul proclaimed, "Now to Him who is able to do exceedingly abundantly beyond all that we ask or imagine, according to the power that works in us, to Him be the glory in the church and in Christ Jesus throughout all generations, forever and ever" (Eph. 3:20–21, MEV).

If you give God five minutes, He will fill it. If you offer Him an hour, He will fill that too. If you give Him twenty-one days of fasting and prayers, He will fill them. And if you offer God your whole life, He will take it and fill it in ways you cannot imagine, because He is the God of capacity. None of us know what we are fully capable of doing when we trust God, not even the greats of the faith such as evangelist D. L. Moody. It is believed that he said the following words to his sons just before he died: "If God be your partner, make your plans large."

God wants you to believe Him for bigger things, to pray and believe for what He knows you are capable of. Believe that this is your season to break through the biggest barriers you have ever faced. When God speaks His Word over your life, believe what you hear and be confident that His Word will change your reality. It doesn't matter what someone else has spoken over your life. What matters is what Jesus says about you. God wants you to have heaven's view of who you really are. Think big, dream big, expect much because there is a divine destiny to your life.

I remember when this happened to me. I was about to celebrate my twentieth birthday when God called me to preach. I recall the moment so clearly—the heavens were opened unto me, and I saw myself preaching, going all over the world sharing the gospel, and that is what has happened in my life because I had faith to believe for it. God loves to be believed! God wants you to know that if you just believe Him, all things are possible. "'For I know the plans I have for you,' declares the LORD, 'plans to prosper you and not to harm you, plans to give you hope and a future'" (Jer. 29:11, NIV). Start right now, believing God for more in your life, and watch what He does!

Chapter Thirteen

DRESS FOR SUCCESS

MUCH HAS BEEN written about the armor of God, because believers understand that spiritual battles need spiritual weapons. God has given us His instructions as to how we are to dress for success by putting on the full armor He provides. Jesus said, "I have given you authority to trample on snakes and scorpions and to overcome all the power of the enemy; nothing will harm you. However, do not rejoice that the spirits submit to you, but rejoice that your names are written in heaven" (Luke 10:19–20, NIV). This promise, given by the Lord, needs to be grasped by *every believer.* When coming against spiritual forces, we must be strong in the Lord and fight with His spiritual weapons.

> Put on the whole armor of God, that you may be able to stand against the wiles of the devil. For we do not wrestle against flesh and blood, but against principalities, against powers, against

the rulers of the darkness of this age, against
spiritual hosts of wickedness in the heavenly
places. Therefore take up the whole armor of
God that you may be able to withstand in the
evil day, and having done all, to stand. Stand
therefore, having girded your waist with truth,
having put on the breastplate of righteousness,
and having shod your feet with the preparation of the gospel of peace; above all, taking
the shield of faith with which you will be able
to quench all the fiery darts of the wicked one.
And take the helmet of salvation, and the sword
of the Spirit, which is the word of God; praying
always with all prayer and supplication in the
Spirit, being watchful to this end with all perseverance and supplication for all the saints.

—EPHESIANS 6:11–18, NKJV

To win against the enemy, we must dress for success.
When Paul was in prison, Roman soldiers guarded
him most of the time, providing a great opportunity
for him to examine all of their armor up close. We
can imagine that as he observed the soldiers, the Holy
Spirit gave Paul the analogy of the armor of God that
we find in Ephesians. Let's take a few moments to
review our spiritual armor, beginning with the belt of
truth. In Ephesians 6:14 Paul said, "Stand firm then,
with the belt of truth buckled around your waist" (NIV).

The belt of truth

In the Roman armor of Paul's day, the belt that went around the soldier's waist was one of the most important pieces of equipment. Everything else the soldier needed in battle was fastened to his belt. If the belt wasn't in place, nothing else was secure. With this in mind, it is easy to understand why Paul tells us that our foundational piece of spiritual armor must be the belt of truth. If we are not grounded in truth through the Scriptures, we will surely fall.

The breastplate of righteousness

The second piece of armor mentioned by Paul in Ephesians is the breastplate of righteousness. In Roman armor the breastplate was made of bronze and usually covered with the tough hide of an animal skin in order to protect the most vital area of the body, the heart. Proverbs 4:23 says, "Keep thy heart with all diligence; for out of it are the issues of life" (KJV). Guarding our hearts has to do with understanding the righteousness of God. "For God made Christ, who never sinned, to be the offering for our sin, so that we could be made right with God through Christ" (2 Cor. 5:21, NLT). The breastplate of His righteousness is a reference to the fact that Satan will attack you and accuse you constantly, therefore, you must rely on Christ's righteousness.

When the devil tries to remind you of your failures,

you can tell him, "It's not my righteousness or works that makes God use me or love me; it's the righteousness that has been given to me through Jesus Christ. Therefore I am righteous in God's sight."

The shoes of peace

Muhammad Ali, perhaps the greatest boxer of all time, had a famous saying: "I float like a butterfly and sting like a bee." Floating like a butterfly was a reference to his footwork. Any boxer knows that if they lose their footing, it is only a matter of time before they are defeated. Anyone who has ever fought in any kind of hand-to-hand combat knows that sure footing is most important. When fighting with swords, as they did in the time of the Roman legions, losing your footing could mean death, so footgear was very important. When fighting face-to-face combat, their feet had to be planted solidly.

Ephesians 6:15 says, "And having shod your feet with the preparation of the gospel of peace" (NKJV). Paul knew that in the Christian life, we would need solid footing. If we are to walk the walk of faith, we will need the shoes of peace to give us solid footing. When the devil tries to knock us off balance, it is the shoes of peace that will enable us to stand firm. When Satan tries to throw worry and anxiety and fear into our life, we just keep on walking with Jesus, wearing the shoes of peace and claiming the promises of

God. Philippians 4:6 says, "Do not be anxious about anything, but in every situation, by prayer and petition, with thanksgiving, present your requests to God" (NIV).

The shield of faith

The next piece of armor from Ephesians is the shield of faith. "In all circumstances take up the shield of faith, with which you can extinguish all the flaming darts of the evil one" (Eph. 6:16, ESV). A Roman soldier's shield was about two feet wide and four feet long. He would use it to ward off the blows of the enemy. Soldiers could hide behind their shields when enemy archers released volleys of arrows, and Roman soldiers could kneel down on the ground and erect a wall of shields around them to block out flaming missiles. As long as you have your shield of faith, Satan's flaming arrows can't get at you with guilt and accusations. Christ in you will give you all the protection you need.

The helmet of salvation

The purpose of a Roman soldier's helmet, just like any soldier's helmet, was, of course, to protect the head, another area that needed to be guarded from a fatal blow. The parallel in our spiritual armor is that the helmet protects our thought life. Too often Christians are tormented in our thought life. The enemy will whisper lies in our ears, telling us we have committed such terrible sins that even God can't forgive them. When we have the helmet of salvation firmly in place, these lies cannot hoodwink us. Our salvation is not dependent upon our performance. It never has been, and it never will be. Our salvation depends on what Jesus did for us, and what He did cannot be undone.

The sword of the Spirit

The last but certainly not the least of the pieces of our spiritual armor is the sword of the Spirit. The sword of the Spirit is the Word of God, and our best offensive weapon in the battle against the powers of darkness. In biblical times a Roman sword had a blade that was twenty-four inches long. Both sides of this blade were sharp, and the end was pointed. We have the Word of God, which is living and sharper than a two-edged sword, and Jesus is our greatest example of how to wield the sword of the Spirit. When He was tempted in the wilderness, He spoke verses of Scripture to Satan to resist his temptations (Luke 4). We are to take God's promises and speak the Word of God and the promises of God like a sword, piercing the lies of the enemy unto defeat.

Put on the full armor

When you get up in the morning, make sure you put on the whole armor of God. Satan attacks us on a daily basis, therefore we need to check our armor daily and make sure it is polished, oiled, and ready for active duty at all times. Ask yourself, "Do I have the belt of truth? Have I read the Word today? Do I have the breastplate of righteousness so I don't slip into a performance relationship with God? Am I wearing shoes that cover me with the peace of God no matter what storms I face?"

Don't allow your sword to get rusty for lack of the Word. Keep it sharp. If you aren't certain of your salvation, then go back to God's Word, get in His presence, and make sure your helmet of salvation is snug on your head. You need the whole armor of God, every day. Take hold of what God has provided, and you will win the battle, every time.

THE BLOOD OF THE LAMB

I have good news for you about the devil: Satan is a lion on a leash! The devil has power, but his power is limited. He appears often as a roaring lion, but this lion is on a leash. Jesus has already defeated him. The blood of the Lamb has been shed for you and for me, for all time. The greatest fear of demons is the blood of Jesus Christ. The application of the shed blood of Jesus Christ spilled on the cross provides our protection and our victory. We overcome him "by the blood of the Lamb and by the word of [our] testimony" (Rev.

12:11, ESV). The devil cannot cross the bloodline. A heart sprinkled with the blood of Jesus Christ is holy ground upon which the devil dares not tread.

The Pilgrim's Progress is considered by some to be the next best-selling book after the Bible. If you haven't yet read it, I encourage you to pick up a copy and read this famous allegory of the Christian life. In the story the character called Christian was approaching a narrow passage as he traveled toward Porter's lodge for the night. In this narrow passage he saw two lions, but didn't realize that they were chained. Very afraid, he considered turning back, until the porter at the lodge, whose name was Watchful, perceived Christian's fear. Crying out in a loud voice, Watchful told Christian not to fear the lions because they were chained and could do him no harm.

Upon hearing Watchful's words, Christian began to cautiously walk into the narrow passage, trembling with fear. As he walked, he could hear the lions roar and feel their hot breath on his flesh, but just as Watchful had said, he was able to pass through unharmed, because the lions were chained. The Bible says, "Resist the devil, and he will flee from you," (James 4:7, MEV). In his book *Satan: His Personality, Power, and Overthrow*, E. M. Bounds said, "Resist means to set one's self against, to withstand. Yield him nothing at any point, but oppose him at every point.

Be always against him, belonging ever to the party of opposition.... Firmness, decision, and opposition, these the devil cannot stand."[1]

Like Christian in *Pilgrim's Progress*, there will be times when we will have to walk through that narrow passage with the devil's breath hot on our flesh, but if we walk with faith in God, we will come out the other side unharmed, because Jesus has already defeated the devil. The walk of faith will get scary at times, but if we are dressed for the journey in the armor of God, victory will be ours in Jesus Christ! "But thanks be to God, who gives us the victory through our Lord Jesus Christ" (1 Cor. 15:57, ESV).

Chapter Fourteen

FREE AT LAST!

THROUGHOUT THIS BOOK I've brought to your attention the story of Paul and Silas in prison because it's the greatest jailbreak story of all time, and it so beautifully illustrates how we too can be free at last from the chains that Satan uses to bind us to sin and death. The Bible says that Paul and Silas had been beaten, falsely accused, stripped, put in chains, and thrown into prison. But that's not the most important part of the story. Yes, they were definitely treated badly. We all get treated badly from time to time in life. There are those around the world who suffer every day for the gospel just as Paul and Silas did.

The most important part of this story isn't how badly they were treated, but how they reacted to what was happening to them. They were falsely accused, beaten, chained, and left to rot in the bottom of a prison cell, but instead of giving in to despair, they chose to hold on to faith and hope, because they knew the One who saves—Jesus Christ. That is the lesson for all of us from this story. Life will falsely accuse us, beat us up, put us in chains of sin, and try and leave us for dead. But like Paul and Silas, we can choose to praise the Lord in our midnight hour.

Our chains are real, but so is God. A chain can be addiction to drugs or alcohol, low self-esteem, fear, depression, eating disorders, pornography addiction, shame, failure. The list goes on and on. But the good news is that we don't have to stay bound by the devil's chains. We can start a "chain reaction" by refusing to give in to addiction, refusing to give in to fear, refusing to give in to an eating disorder, to shame. We don't have to embrace the lies of the enemy. We don't have to give him control over our life. Like Paul and Silas, we can decide how we want to respond.

Satan wants you to think you don't have any options, but we always have options in Christ. He is our option! When we choose Jesus, our chains begin to break off. Paul and Silas were chained up, beaten up, messed up, and treated unfairly, but at midnight they prayed and sang praises unto God. That's the proper "chain reaction." People sometimes wonder why I praise the Lord like I do—with my hands lifted up and shouts of praise. I get exuberant about my praise as a chain reaction to the chains that Satan tries to bind me with. You can do the same. You can have a chain reaction every time the devil tries to push you down with his lies. When you feel the hot hand of the enemy on your back, start praising God! Declare that He is on the throne, that you will not give in to worry or fear, but instead you will trust the Lord, for He is good and His mercies endure forever.

The Bible says the other prisoners heard Paul and Silas praising God. Sometimes you're not praising God for yourself, not worshipping and making noise for yourself, but for the people around you who are in chains and need to hear your praise. They need you to set an example of what a chain reaction looks like.

The Bible says that when the power and presence of God hit that jailhouse, it rocked; it experienced an earthquake! The building was rocked to its foundation, everyone's shackles were loosed, and every prison door was opened. Now that's what I call a jailhouse rock! Everyone in that prison was set free by the chain reaction started by Paul and Silas. What God did for them, He will do for you. He is the same yesterday, today, and forever!

Break Free!

So often when we're oppressed by the devil and don't know how to fight back, we eventually just begin to wear the chains he puts on us. We actually begin to believe the lies of the enemy. A spiritual "Stockholm syndrome" takes hold of us and binds us to our captor. For those who are not familiar with the Stockholm syndrome, it is the name of a study that was done in Stockholm, Sweden, in 1973, which concluded that victims of crimes can develop an emotional attachment for their captors if they are held captive long enough. They actually begin to accept their bondage.

That's what the devil wants to accomplish in us—to make us accept his bondage, by wearing us down, beating us down, until we just give in to hopelessness and despair, until we become so accustomed to failure, to losing, to defeat that we begin to embrace these things. "I have a right to be depressed," some will say. "I have a right to be fearful." The truth is, that's not true! You don't have to own the lies of the devil. God wants you to take ownership of His truths. Where the Spirit of the Lord is, there is freedom; freedom from worry, fear, depression, defeat, and lies; freedom to live a limitless life with Jesus Christ.

In Acts 12 it says that Peter was in prison, and they chained his hands and his feet. Then it goes on to say that *a light shone into his prison.* That's what I'm doing right now for every one of you reading this book. I'm writing these words to deliver a message from God, and a light is shining into whatever prison you may be in. You may be chained by the enemy is some area of your life, but the light of God's Word is shining in your life right now.

When that light shone into Paul's prison cell, it was the light of God's presence and with it came an angel. The next thing Peter knew, the angel said, "Come on, let's get out of here." And Scripture says that *when he got up, his chains fell off.* Did you catch that? When Paul got up, his chains fell off. Paul stood against the onslaught of the enemy and saw his problems fall away. But not only did Paul have to stand, he also had to have faith to follow the angel out of that prison. That's what God wants you to understand. If you're bound by addiction, drugs, alcohol, depression, or any other chains of the enemy, God has burst open your prison! The light is shining, but you have to follow where He's leading. You have to do your part. You have to have a chain reaction. You have to say, "I refuse these chains, and I will not be an addict. And when I get free, the same freedom is going touch my family, it's going touch my friends, it's going be a chain reaction."

This chain reaction starts with you, but it doesn't have to stop with you. God will keep the blessings flowing until your entire family is saved. He's calling you to freedom, and it's not just for you. You are the one God will use to orchestrate a jailbreak for your entire family. When they see the change in you, the ones who are bound in the same chains are going to want what you have, and you will be able to show them how to get it. If God's miracles can happen in your life, they can happen for your family as well.

If you are reading this right now and you have chains in your life, hear the Word of God. "'For I know the plans I have for you' declares the LORD, 'plans to prosper you and not to harm you, plans to give you hope and a future'" (Jer. 29:11, NIV). If there is anything going through your mind that doesn't give you hope, it's time to stand up, watch those chains fall off, and follow God out of that prison. You can be a different person than you were when you started reading this book. You can say, "Whatever happens, God is *with* me, God is *for* me, God is *in* me, and it's going be all right."

If this is you, I want you to picture those chains that are wrapped around your life—anything that has been limiting you, holding you back—and as you pray this prayer, watch those chains fall away.

> *Lord Jesus, I surrender my life to You now. No more chains. Break every chain in my life that has been holding me back from all that You have for me. Set me free. Give me a brand-new life. I don't want to be chained to the pain of the past. I don't want to be bound up by the devil. I give*

everything over to You. Wash me. Cleanse me. I'm ready to follow my angel out of bondage into a place of freedom. I receive my freedom, for he whom the Son sets free is free indeed. I receive freedom from [say whatever you need to break free from right now]. *I am no longer the prey of the devil. Lord Jesus, this is my chain reaction. In Jesus's name, amen.*

FILLED WITH THE SPIRIT

T HE LOS ANGELES area of California has a serious pollution problem. Several years ago an environmental expert was commissioned to conduct an extensive study on what Los Angeles could do about this issue. Massive amounts of money were spent on researching the problem. Finally, the expert called everyone together to report his findings. He surprised everyone when he proclaimed that after all his research he had concluded that there was no solution to their pollution problem. Can you imagine that?

But something really jumped out at me as I read this story. The newspaper said that after sharing his report and coming to the conclusion that there was no solution, the expert paused and said these words like an afterthought: "What you really need is *a wind from elsewhere* to come and sweep through the city and blow all of this pollution out to sea." Now, when I heard the phrase *"wind from elsewhere,"* the preacher in me saw a clear spiritual parallel. When we look at our current spiritual condition, there is definitely pollution, and we don't have to look far to find it. The church is polluted, and it's not the first time.

In the Bible the Book of Malachi opens with an examination of the pollution that had crept into the lives of God's people. They had fallen into wickedness, idolatry, and sin. Their animal sacrifices were polluted, revealing the condition of their hearts. Animal sacrifice in the Old Testament was designed to sweep away sin so that God's people could live under His protection and favor. But their sacrifices had become so polluted that God finally refused to accept them anymore. Then He went on to say He would smite the earth with a curse because of their sins and hardheartedness.

God's chosen people had become so polluted with sin, adultery, idolatry and corruption that He stopped speaking to them. For the next four hundred years, between the close of the Old Testament and beginning of the New Testament, God was silent. There was no one alive that we know of who had an encounter with God during this spiritually dark time. The pollution of sin was thick and heavy on the human race.

But then, on the Day of Pentecost, there came that *wind from elsewhere*. "When the Day of Pentecost had fully come...suddenly there came a sound from heaven, as of a rushing mighty wind" (Acts 2:1–2, NKJV). It filled the Upper Room. It filled the church that had become formal and religious but had lost its intensity and passion for God. When God breathed that *wind from elsewhere* in Acts 2, verse 1, it began to sweep out all the pollution, all the corruption, all the iniquity and sin that had built up since the days of Malachi. Scripture tells us that there were 120 people gathered in the Upper Room on the Day of Pentecost. I see them as representative of the generations who had been cursing, lying, cheating, and stealing. When that *wind from elsewhere* hit them, it swept all the uncleanliness right out of their lives and into a sea of forgetfulness where it was remembered no more.

The church today needs a *wind from elsewhere*; our cities need it, and our hearts need it too. We need God's cleansing Spirit to blow in and clean things out. Your sin pollution can't be fixed by "experts." You need the wind of the Holy Spirit to sweep you clean and make you a new creation, to sweep sins such as alcohol or sexual immorality right out of you forever! "'Not by might nor by power, but by My Spirit,' says the LORD of Hosts" (Zech. 4:6, MEV). When the wind of the Holy Spirit comes, He will cleanse your heart, and your spirit, and your mind from the pollution and filth of this world.

This *wind from elsewhere* will make you fast and pray. It will make you read your Bible. It will make you live right. Sometimes we just can't go any further until we say, "Lord, set me free. Lord, give me liberty again. Lord, send a wind!" And you don't just need that *wind from elsewhere* one time; the enemy certainly isn't going to give up and go away. You're going to need the Holy Spirit to come through every once in a while and sweep away your old ways and your old thinking. When you feel the hot hand of the devil on your life, that's when you need *a wind from elsewhere* to sweep away your carnality and your lust.

Some of you have gone too long without God's wind blowing through your life. It's been too long since you let yourself become broken before God with tears streaming down your face. Perhaps you don't pray anymore or read your Bible anymore. Whatever it is that's causing you to sin, you need *a wind from elsewhere* to blow through our life. And when it does, watch out! It will make you love God more! It will make you wake up in the middle of the night and feel angels in the room. When God breaks you free from the enemy's grip, you will feel glad to be alive!

On Fire for God, Passionate for Jesus

At the turn of the century students in Charles Parham's Bethel Bible School in Topeka, Kansas, couldn't seem to get off the topic of whether or not the Holy Spirit could still come like a "mighty rushing wind" and fill people causing them to "speak with other tongues, as the Spirit gave them utterance" (Acts 2:2, 4, NKJV). No matter what class they were in, the subject always came up. Finally, their hunger became so intense that they decided to declare a fast for the close of 1900 going into the New Year. They all agreed that they would fast and pray for God to fill them with the same Holy Spirit power found in chapter 2 of the Book of Acts.

God heard them and answered their prayers. On New Year's Day 1901 suddenly there came a wind from elsewhere. A young woman began speaking in Chinese, followed by many others who all spoke in different languages. At least twenty-one known languages were spoken and verified by native speakers who began to show up at many of their meetings. These events became known as the *Topeka Outpouring*.

But God didn't stop with the students. In 1905 Lucy Farrow, a former slave, spent two months with the Parham family in Topeka. At the time Farrow was leading a small Holiness church in Houston, Texas, and was hungry for an Acts 2 encounter with God. Leaving William J. Seymour in charge of her flock in Houston, she headed for Topeka, where she encountered more of God. Eventually Charles Parham and his family would follow Lucy back to Houston to set up a Bible school similar to their Bethel School in Topeka.

Seymour, who had been on his own quest for an

encounter with the Holy Spirit, attended Parham's Bible school in Houston, and by early 1906 Seymour accepted an invitation to lead a congregation in Los Angeles, California. Although he still had not personally had an experience of speaking in tongues, he was profoundly affected by the teaching of Parham. Upon his arrival in Los Angeles, Seymour began to preach about the power of the Holy Spirit and speaking in tongues. When the doors of his congregation's meeting place were padlocked shut, he began to fast and pray, hoping he would soon experience a powerful spiritual encounter. Hours turned into days, and others began to join him in his vigil.

Edward Lee, a janitor at a local bank who attended Seymour's church, showed up at one of the vigil meetings where he had a powerful vision of Peter and Paul shaking under the power of the Holy Ghost. When he shared this vision with the prayer group, Seymour, feeling led of God, laid his hands on his friend to pray for him. Lee's legs buckled, and he fell to the ground under the power of God. Seymour knew something profound had just begun. *A wind from elsewhere* had begun to blow.

Continuing his vigil of fasting and prayer, and in need of more space, Seymour relocated his congregation to 312 Azusa Street in Los Angeles. It was there at Azusa Street that revival broke out that went on day and night for three and a half years. The modern-day Pentecostal movement was birthed out of the wind from elsewhere that blew through 312 Azusa Street. People came from all over the world to attend Seymour's meetings. Several major denominations with churches around the world are in existence today as a result of Seymour's prevailing prayer and fasting for *a wind from elsewhere.*[1]

Being very familiar with the great outpouring at Azusa Street, when I heard an expert telling city officials in Los Angeles that what they really needed was a "wind from elsewhere," my ears pricked up. I would like to have been in that meeting, when the expert made his announcement, because I would have stood up and said, "Sir, I can take you to a place in Los Angeles where the 'wind' came. And if you can tap into this 'wind,' it will sweep the gangs out of Los Angeles; it will sweep prostitution out. It will clean up Hollywood. It will clean up our nation!"

We are in desperate need of a wind from elsewhere in this whole country right now, not just in Los Angeles. We need it to clean up our cities, sweep out the gangs, drugs, child abusers, murderers, and all the other sin problems that have no earthly solution. Our dedicated law-enforcement entities work hard, but they cannot stem the tide of spiritual pollution that is upon us. Only God can clean things up. Only God can send His Holy Spirit to bring hearts to repentance and new life.

The same Holy Spirit of God that put the dry bones together in Ezekiel can put us back together, stand us on our feet, and make us into a great army of believers who partner with God so that His will may be done on earth as it is in heaven. The Holy Spirit has all power in heaven and earth, and when He starts moving, anything is possible. When the Holy Spirit is moving, you can prosper in a famine, gain while others are losing, regain what was lost, and more! That's the power of God for His people whose hearts are steadfast.

If you are in the midst of tough times and feel like you're down for the count and will never get up again, I'm here to tell you—that's not true! You *can* get up again. The Lord has a word for you—He has a wind from elsewhere that can put you on your feet again, no matter how dry your bones are. He can come right in to that valley you're in and put your back together and set you on your feet and lead you into a limitless life, if you'll let Him. It's time for you to receive *a wind from elsewhere* to sweep away everything that's not of Jesus in your life. It's time to break free from the grip of the devil and breathe in the fresh air—to breathe in the wind of the Holy Spirit.

How long has it been since you had *a wind from elsewhere* filling up your life? Ask God to fill you with the Holy Ghost, and He'll clean up your house, clean up your family, and clean up your attitude. If you are angry or bitter toward anyone, you need *a wind from elsewhere* to sweep the religion right out of you. It will sweep prejudice out of you. It will sweep hate out of you. It will sweep anger and offense right out the door, and make room for God's Holy Spirit to take up residence in you. None of us has an answer for the pollution of sin in our lives. We can't fix it, only God can.

If you are reading this and do not have a personal relationship with Jesus Christ, I encourage you to stop right now and confess your sin to Him. Ask His forgiveness, and invite Him into your life. That's the first step. If you have already done this, but are desperate for a fresh encounter with God, it is time to close this book and have an old-fashioned Holy Ghost revival right now, right where you are, just you and the Holy Spirit. It's not hard—all you have to do is hunger and thirst for Him and humble yourself, and He will come.

The wind of the Spirit blows where there is the least resistance. Have you ever noticed how wind will whip through alleys? That's because it can't go through buildings, so it finds ways around, different directions. When you stand on the shore of a lake or the ocean, there is typically a lot of wind because the atmosphere is wide open—there is nothing to block the wind. God is waiting for you to be wide open to Him, to take down any barriers to the wind of His Spirit that He wants to blow through your life. Begin to ask God for a fresh touch of His Holy Spirit in your life. Open yourself up and let the wind blow!

It doesn't matter who you are, what your age or occupation, whether you've never been to church or been a faithful churchgoer for years. None of that matters to God. He doesn't care if you're a pastor or ministry leader. If you haven't had a mighty encounter with God in a long time, now's the time! Do whatever it takes to get in position and catch His wind from elsewhere.

Writing this book has caused a stirring in my spirit, giving rise to the hope that your spirit has been stirred as well; stirred to a life of hope, a life without limits in the power of the Spirit. Stirred to a life free from the bondage of sin, free to prosper in every way. I would like to end with the words of Paul in his letter to the Corinthians, urging you to come boldly before God, seeking His face and the wind of His Holy Spirit so that your life may be made radiant as you are transformed more and more into His likeness.

> Seeing then that we have such hope, we speak
> with great boldness, not as Moses, who put a
> veil over his face, so that the children of Israel
> could not look intently at the end of what was

fading away.... But we all, seeing the glory of the Lord with unveiled faces, as in a mirror, are being transformed into the same image from glory to glory by the Spirit of the Lord.

—2 CORINTHIANS 3:12–13, 18, MEV

NOTES

CHAPTER THIRTEEN: DRESS FOR SUCCESS

1. E. M. Bounds, *Satan: His Personality, Power, and Overthrow* (N.p.: Fleming H. Revell, 1922), 137. Viewed at Google Books.

CONCLUSION: FILLED WITH THE SPIRIT

1. Craig Borlase, *William Seymour: A Biography* (Lake Mary, FL: Charisma House, 2006), 57–127.

CONNECT WITH US!